W9-CHV-946

ROSES

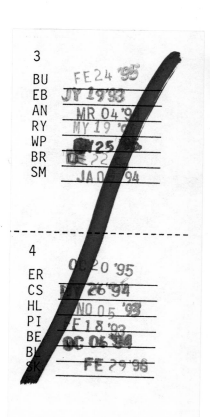

ROSES

Cathy Wilkinson Barash

CHARTWELL
BOOKS, INC.

372 8300

This book was designed and produced by
Quintet Publishing Limited
6 Blundell Street
London N7 9BH

Creative Director: Terry Jeavons
Art Director: Ian Hunt
Designer: Annie Moss
Project Editor: Judith Simons
Editor: Karin Fancett
Photographer: Cathy Wilkinson Barash

Typeset in Great Britain by
Central Southern Typesetters, Eastbourne
Manufactured in Hong Kong by
Regent Publishing Services Limited
Printed in Hong Kong by
Leefung-Asco Printers Limited

Acknowledgements

*Thanks to all whose help has been invaluable to this project: Ellen
Minet for patiently digging, planting and pruning; Maggie Oster and
Susan Roth for lending help and support; the Long Island Rose Society
for allowing me to photograph their rose show; Rizz Arthur for giving
me her rose garden to grow as I wished – organically; Bob Titus for
sharing his garden and love of the rose; Toodie Walt for generously
transporting me to rose gardens day after day; and especially Bill Barash
for posing, proofreading, copying and caring.*

CONTENTS

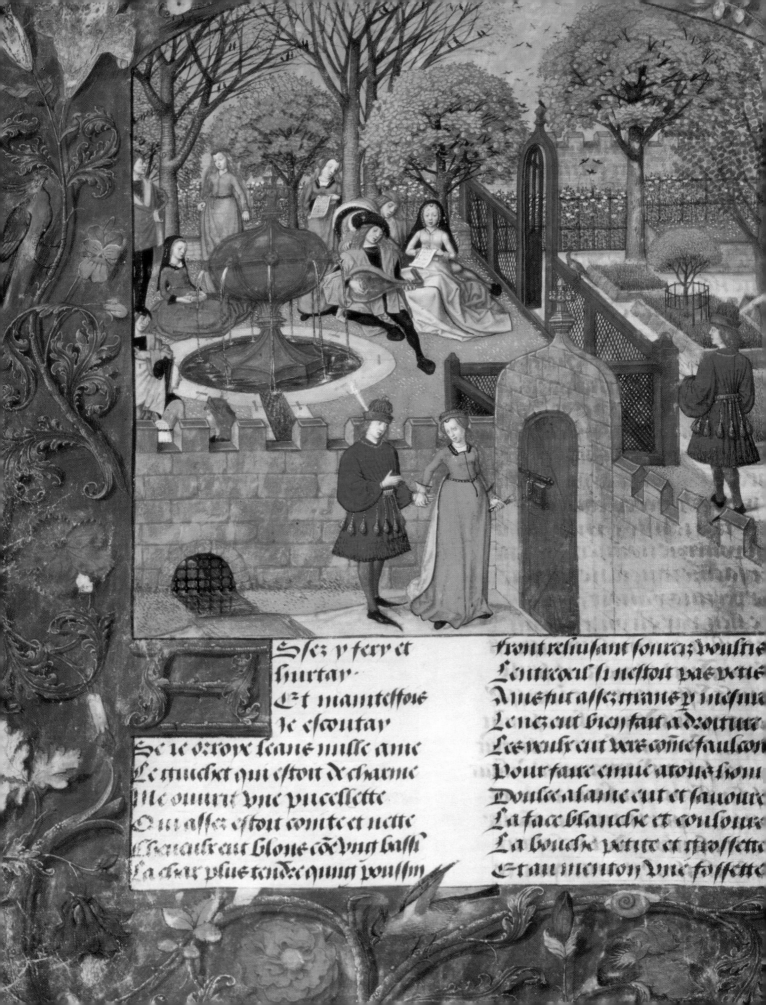

Sse; y ferr et
shirtay.
Et maintesfois
ie escoutay.
Se le otoix seaue mille ame
Le truchet qui estoit de charme
Ille ourrit vne pucellette
Ou masse estoit comte et nette
Les cheuaulx eut blone come vng bassi
La char plus tendre quug poussin

hont reliusant souvez voultie
Lentreoul si nestoit pas petis
Ame fut asse; mais y mesma
Lenes eut bien fait adroiture
Les veulx eut vrie come faulson
Pour faire enuie aroute sion
Douse alaine eut et sauoure
La face blanche et conlouree
La bouche petite et estrossette
Et au menton vne fossette

INTRODUCTION

Roses are among the most ancient of flowers and are one of the most revered. There is fossil evidence indicating that roses have been on the Earth for over 40 million years, certainly predating humans. Yet people and roses have formed a bond that has not been broken throughout recorded time. Roses are native to all parts of the world north of the Equator. Although they grow splendidly in the Southern Hemisphere, none are indigenous to the southern latitudes.

OPPOSITE Roses were an important element in medieval literature and gardens, as can be seen from this page of the original 15th-century manuscript version of La Romaunt de la Rose, *by Guillaume de Lorris. The roses of the title can be seen climbing the trellis in the background.*
~

Roses throughout history

Today, we can find relics of the ancient roses in diverse forms. On the island of Crete between 2800 and 2100 BC, the Minoans re-created the beauty of rose in their jewellery. Aphrodite

BELOW Roses were greatly prized by the Romans and are seen here growing among fruit trees in a fresco painting from the Empress Livia's villa, Rome, c.1st-century AD.
~

ABOVE *'Emilia in her Garden' from* Master of the Hours of Burgundy, c.1465. Rosa gallica, *the Red Rose of Lancaster, and* Rosa alba, *the White Rose of York, climb the trellis of this typical enclosed medieval garden.*
~

anointed Hector with rose oil in Homer's *Iliad*. Confucius (551 to 479 BC) wrote about the cultivation of roses in his day. At that time they were grown in the Imperial Gardens of the Chou Dynasty. People's intervention with nature, as far as the rose is concerned, goes back much further. It is believed that the rose was first cultivated during the Shen Nung Dynasty in China, about 2737 to 2697 BC, and reached a degree of great sophistication during the Han dynasties from 206 BC to 9 AD.

While the Western world was not attracted to the rose until much later in history, it soon became obsessed with the flower. Although the Greeks grew roses about 2,000 years ago, it was the Romans who first seriously cultivated them. Their attraction to roses was not just for their fragrance and beauty, but also for their purported medicinal properties. Early on in the Romans' love affair with the rose, the flowers were imported from Egypt. However, the supply could not keep up with the ever-increasing demand. Logically, the Romans began to cultivate roses themselves. With the same creative genius that built the great aqueducts and viaducts, they created the first greenhouses using hot water pipes to keep the plants warm enough to bloom in winter. Roses flourished with the Roman Empire. Those who could afford to, carpeted their homes with rose petals and even made beds from rose petals. The flowers perfumed the baths. Roman women knew that the essence of the roses made them smell good, but also believed it to have anti-ageing properties, so used it as a skin emollient.

The rose went into a decline with the fall of Rome. It was looked upon by the church as a symbol of the Roman excesses. For nearly a thousand years, roses were cultivated only in the odd monastery. By the 1200s, the church reversed itself, in fact embracing the symbolism of the rose – white for the Virgin Mary's Immaculate Conception, and red (the briar rose) for Christ's blood. Rose beads were traditionally made from a heated mixture of cut up rose petals, salt and water that was rolled out to the desired shape. Such beads were strung together to form a rosary, which translates as a 'gathering of roses'.

Political roses

Roses have had a long history politically. In the days of the Roman Empire, if a rose were hung from the ceiling during a meeting, it signified that nothing was to be revealed about the matters discussed, it was to be secret – *sub rosa*. In the early Catholic Church, the confessional often had a white rose painted above the entrance, or a bouquet of white roses nearby signifying confidentiality of the confessional.

Roses have even been symbolic in battle. In the Wars of the Roses, fought in England from 1455 to 1485, the House of York was represented by the white rose, while the House of Lancaster

ABOVE A Turkish maiden arranges a profusion of tea roses and other garden flowers in The Bey's Garden, *by J F Lewis, 1865. Tea roses – so called since their scent echoes that of freshly crushed tea leaves – were first introduced from China to Europe during the late 18th century.*
~

was represented by the red rose: the two houses fought bitterly for the English crown. Peace finally came when Elizabeth of York wed Henry Tudor of Lancaster establishing the joint House of Tudor. Legend has it that just before the wedding and peace was to be declared, there sprang up a new rose with white petals flecked with red. With the houses united the Tudor rose or York and Lancaster rose *(Rosa damascena versicolor)* became the national emblem of England. The unification is also symbolized with a red and a white rose entwined.

Napoleon Bonaparte's first wife, the Empress Josephine, can be credited with the first international collection of roses which she grew in the gardens of her home at Malmaison, situated just outside of Paris. The gardens were designed not only to show off the blooms, but the characteristics of the plants as well. Josephine cultivated all 256 varieties known at that time, including Bourbon, centifolia, China, damask, gallica, moss, Noisette and rugosa. From crosses and backcrosses of these roses over the ensuing years have come the roses that we are familiar with today: hybrid perpetuals (1837), hybrid teas (1867), polyanthas (1875), floribundas (1924) and grandifloras (1954).

Roses in the Arts

Roses have provided inspiration for many art forms. *Rosa damascena,* the Damask rose, first arrived in Europe with the great commerce that began with the Crusades in the 12th century. However, this rose was introduced in literature by Virgil in 50 BC. Roses have been referred to and written about by writers and poets too numerous to mention in everything from love sonnets to eulogies.

The Provence rose *(Rosa centifolia),* cultivated from the Middle Ages, was a favourite in Flemish and Dutch still life paintings of the 17th and 18th centuries. Empress Josephine's roses at Malmaison have been preserved in the magnificent paintings of Pierre Joseph Redouté in his folio *Les Roses.* Roses wound their way into architecture as well. The rose was featured in architectural details by the ancient Assyrians and Babylonians. Their form was also the inspiration for the great rose windows which grace such magnificent medieval cathedrals as the one at Chartres, France.

The Victorians perfected the language of roses. A gentleman and lady could express a wide range of sentiments which were conveyed by roses. Not only did the colour have significance, but also the arrangement of the leaves, buds and blooms gave a short message. Much of this has been lost, but some of the symbolism remains today.

ABOVE Still Life of Roses, Tulips and Other Flowers, *Roelandt Savery, Holland, 17th century. Roses, in particular Provence roses, were favourite subjects in Flemish and Dutch still life paintings of the 17th and 18th centuries.*
~

Beginnings of the modern roses

The year 1789 was a pivotal one for the rose. Prior to that time, roses bloomed once, for a short time only. In that decisively important year, the China rose first came to France and England. It had the unique quality of blooming for several months at a time. The tea rose soon followed, also from the Orient. These two roses are the ancestors of today's hybrid tea roses.

The Queen of Flowers, present and future

It was the Ancient Greek poet Sappho who gave roses the appellation 'Queen of Flowers' more than 2,500 years ago. The strong bonds between humans and roses, having lasted for millennia, will no doubt continue into the next millenium. If given a choice of plants to put in a garden, most people would pick the rose. Although its beauty may be fleeting, especially in some of its northern ranges, it is indelible. To me, there is nothing quite as beautiful as the first flush of colour on the first rose in spring, nor quite as sweet as the smell of the last rose before the frost.

With modern technology such as gene splicing and cloning, who can tell what the future of roses will be? Breeders and hybridizers have been working on disease-resistant varieties for a number of years. Perhaps someday we will see an ever-blooming (year-round), large-flowered, frost-resistant, fragrant, pest and disease-resistant, thornless rose which changes its colour over the season. Yet that would take all the fun out of growing roses, for, to me, the joy is in the challenge – growing a vigorous rose without chemicals, discovering a new fragrance or a new colour, and getting my hands into the soil and becoming one with the rose and the earth.

ABOVE The rose has provided inspiration for many art forms, including the great rose windows such as 'La Rose de France' in the 13-century cathedral at Chartres, France.

~

THE SYMBOLISM OF ROSES

COLOUR	SENTIMENT EXPRESSED
Red	Love, respect
Deep pink	Gratitude, appreciation
Light pink	Admiration, sympathy
White	Reverence, humility
Yellow	Joy, gladness
Orange	Enthusiasm, desire
Red and yellow blend	Gaiety, joviality
Pale blended tones	Sociability, friendship

CULTIVATION

To grow roses well, follow these four guidelines:

1 Choose a location with at least four to six hours of direct sun a day, good air circulation, and away from trees and large shrubs that shade roses and compete for soil nutrients.

2 Select good plant material with at least three healthy canes.

3 Provide good soil and good drainage.

4 Give the plant a lot of TLC (tender loving care). This includes mulching, feeding, watering, weeding, pruning, preparing the plant for winter dormancy, and controlling pests and diseases.

OPPOSITE Admire the roses in your neighbourhood and ask fellow gardeners for advice before purchasing new rose stock.
~

ROSE ANATOMY – SHOOT & ROOT STRUCTURE

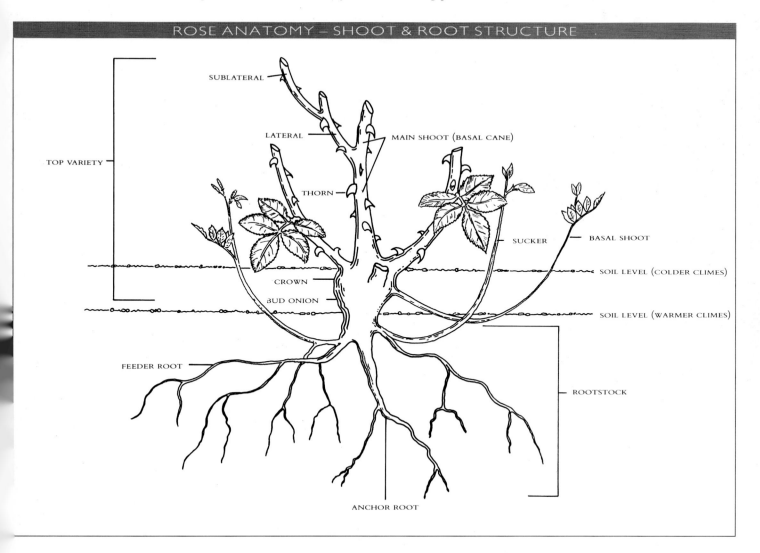

TOP VARIETY

SUBLATERAL

LATERAL

MAIN SHOOT (BASAL CANE)

THORN

SUCKER

BASAL SHOOT

SOIL LEVEL (COLDER CLIMES)

CROWN

BUD ONION

SOIL LEVEL (WARMER CLIMES)

FEEDER ROOT

ROOTSTOCK

ANCHOR ROOT

SELECTING A ROSE

To paraphrase Gertrude Stein, a rose is not a rose is not a rose. With thousands in cultivation today, the choice is not whether or not to buy a rose, but which one(s) to choose. Considering the number of varieties available, that decision can seem mind-boggling indeed. There are roses for almost every climate. A number of roses have been bred for disease resistance. Some roses need more attention than others. Before setting out to purchase a rose, whether from a garden centre, nursery or from a reputable mail-order company, do a little research. Read through the A–Z section of this book to help select the right rose for you and your garden.

The information in books and catalogues is invaluable, and it is also helpful to see a plant in its own setting. Take a walk around your neighbourhood, admiring the roses and asking about their cultivation. Most gardeners are pleased to have their efforts noticed and are willing to share information; it is also a good way to meet new friends. A visit to a botanic garden or

ABOVE For inspiration, visit a local botanical garden to view roses in a variety of settings. A rose arbour, such as this, can be reproduced on a smaller scale in a domestic garden.
~

ROSES FOR THE NOVICE GARDENER

The following varieties are some of the easiest roses to grow and ideal for the inexperienced rose gardener.

'America' (Cl)	'Green Ice' (Min)
'Bewitched' (HT)	'Mister Lincoln' (HT)
'Charlotte Armstrong' (HT)	'Pink Parfait' (Gr)
'Cinderella' (Min)	'Queen Elizabeth' (Gr)
'Europeana' (F)	'Rise 'n' Shine' (Min)
'Fragrant Cloud' (HT)	'Shreveport' (Gr)
'Futura' (HT)	'The Fairy' (Pol)

KEY: F — FLORIBUNDA GR — GRANDIFLORA HT — HYBRID TEA CI — CLIMBER MIN — MINIATURE POL — POLYANTHA

arboretum is well worth the time during the rose season. Roses can be seen in a variety of settings in a botanic garden – a formal rose garden, on an arbour or fence, in an informal garden setting, or even as specimen plants.

After deciding which rose(s) to buy, the next decision is whether to purchase them at a nursery or by mail. There are advantages and disadvantages to each. A mail-order company has a larger selection than a nursery or garden centre, but you cannot pick and choose between plants of the same variety as you can at a nursery. The advantage in purchasing a rose from a nursery is that it can be added to the garden immediately, while there is a delay between placing a mail-order and receiving and planting the rose.

Grades of roses

It does not pay to skimp when purchasing a rose; you get what you pay for. When buying a rose, it is important to check the grade, which must be listed in a catalogue or on a plant. All roses are graded for quality based on their size and growth when packaged, whether bare-root or container grown. The top-graded roses are usually two-year-old field-grown plants with at least three strong canes 9.5mm (⅜in) in diameter or larger. Middle grade roses are generally younger and less sturdy than top grade ones, but can grow into good plants with time and attention. The lowest grade roses require a lot of time and attention to become good specimen plants, but are useful in mass plantings, as background plants or hedges, as they are the least expensive to purchase.

Bare-root roses

Most plants from mail-order companies are dormant, bare-root roses. They are kept in cold storage and sent to the buyer at the proper time for planting (early spring in colder climates, or late autumn or winter in areas where there is no danger of frost).

Some nurseries and garden centres have a limited number of bare-root roses in early spring. Be sure the plants have been stored in a cool, moist environment. Inspect the canes to be sure they are healthy with a green or reddish colour and are firm to the touch. Do not purchase bare-root plants that have dry-looking or dead canes. Bare-root roses should be dormant. Do not accept plants that have broken dormancy with a lot of new growth.

Container-grown roses

Container-grown roses are sold at nurseries, garden centres, and even at some supermarkets. Miniature roses can be found year-

ABOVE Visit nurseries and garden centres for container-grown roses (background). These outlets also stock a limited selection of bare-root roses (foreground) in early spring, but a wider range of varieties can be purchased through mail-order companies.

~

round, while other varieties are only for sale during the growing season. The choice of container-grown plants is very limited compared to bare-root plants and are often more expensive to buy. Container-grown roses are available later in the season, so they can be purchased in bloom. At that time, the vigour of the plant is more obvious, even to the novice's eye. Obviously, what you see is what you get as far as colour is concerned. Sometimes the colour of a rose in a catalogue varies from what you see on a plant actually in bloom, due to limitations in colour reproduction with some printing processes.

Container-grown roses come in plastic pots, metal cans or cardboard, corrugated paper or fibre containers. They must be transplanted into the garden. Miniatures and some small tree roses purchased in plain or decorative pots can remain in these containers.

SOIL COMPONENTS

ORGANIC MATTER

WATER

CLAY

SILT

SAND

ABOVE An alternative method of assessing soil type is to mix top soil and water in a jar and leave it to settle overnight. The components will separate out and the proportions will indicate the type of soil. If the layer of silt is equal to the layers of clay and sand your soil is a good loam.

~

SOIL PREPARATION

Soil is not just dirt; it is a living substance with various biological, chemical and physical forces constantly at work. There are five major components to soil: air, living organisms (from microscopic bacteria, viruses and fungi to earthworms and insects), humus (organic material in varying states of decay), water, and inorganic particles of minerals and rocks.

Soil types

Soil is classified by the size of the inorganic particles as sand, silt or clay. Most garden soil is a mixture of the three. Laboratory testing can determine the exact soil composition, but, for most gardeners, soil type can be determined right there in the garden. Gently squeeze a small amount of soil in your hand, then rub it between your fingers. Sandy soil has the largest particles, does not stay together when squeezed, and feels gritty to the touch. Easy to work, it drains very well, but water draining through removes most of the nutrients. Silt is midway in size between sand and clay, with a smooth texture. It can be squeezed together, but does not remain compacted, especially when dry. Clay, known as heavy soil, absorbs and holds a tremendous amount of moisture. The particles are so fine that it holds its shape when compressed, but does not allow for air or water movement. Good soil is often called loam, and is a mixture of the three types. Rub it between your fingers and it breaks up into smaller particles. It holds moisture well and encourages the biological activity that is necessary for healthy soil.

Amending soil

Soil is the major source of food and water for a rose. Take the time to choose a proper location and prepare the soil well before planting. The highest quality rose, if planted in poor soil, will not thrive. Conversely a poor quality rose planted in good soil enriched with organic matter will flourish. Three characteristics of good soil are good drainage, plenty of humus, and an abundance of nutrients available to the plant.

If planting an entire bed with roses, it is worth the time and effort to improve the soil in the bed before planting. If planting a single rose, only the soil around the root area needs to be worked.

Most soils can benefit from the addition of organic material. Turn the soil, breaking up any large clods. For every 10 square metres of garden, add about 2kg of superphosphate and 5 to 7.5kg of well-rotted manure, compost, dehydrated bird manure, peat moss, leaf mould, or shredded bark. (This is roughly the same as 4lb of superphosate and 10 to 15lb manure or similar per 100 per sq ft.) Turn this into the soil and dig in well. To get a head start next spring, prepare a new bed in the autumn, so that roses can be planted as soon as the ground can be worked again at the end of winter.

pH – soil acidity and alkalinity

Soil pH in the range of 6.0 to 6.5, or slightly acid, is ideal for growing roses. pH is a numerical measure of acidity and alkalinity, with a range from 0 (most acid) to 14 (most alkaline) with 7 neutral. If the soil pH is not right for a particular plant, it cannot get the nutrients it needs from the soil. Amend soil well before planting and it is not necessary to worry about soil pH when planting new roses. Check the pH of established beds, especially any that border a lawn area. When lawns are limed to raise the pH, the pH in adjoining beds is often raised as the lime leaches through the soil. Simple kits for pH testing are available at garden centres and nurseries. As a customer service, some nurseries will test soil pH. If the soil tests alkaline, add aluminium sulphate at the prescribed rate to bring the pH into the acceptable range. If the soil tests too acid, add granulated limestone to raise the pH to the proper level. Follow the package instructions for the rate of application.

PLANTING

Roses grown in containers

Container-grown roses are easier to plant than bare-root roses. Dig a hole somewhat bigger than the container. Amend the soil as above. Add about 15cm (6in) of soil to the hole. The package directions for roses in cardboard or fibre containers say to plant the rose container and all, but roses do better if their roots are not restricted by a container. Remove the rose from the container, keeping the surrounding soil intact as much as possible. Position the rose at the same soil level as it was in the container. Add soil, filling the hole half-way. Gently firm the soil so that any air pockets are eliminated. Add the rest of the soil and water well. Usually container-grown roses are actively growing, so do not need to be mounded as do bare-root plants. Mulch and keep well watered until the plant is firmly established.

ABOVE Miniature roses grow well in containers. This one has been trained in a tree form and planted with alyssum, petunias and pansies for an attractive garden centrepiece.

~

Spacing plants

Allow at least 30cm (1ft) between miniature roses, 60cm (2ft) between hybrid teas, 75cm (2½ft) between grandifloras, 90cm (3ft) between floribundas, 1.2m (4ft) between standards and 2.1m (7ft) between climbers. Roses should not be planted closer than 45cm (18in) to the edges of the border or bed. Adequate spacing not only allows for good air circulation, thus preventing fungal diseases, and keeps plants from touching, preventing the spread of disease from plant to plant, but most importantly gives you access to each plant. There is nothing worse than trying to tend a tightly planted rose garden, and becoming hopelessly entangled on thorns.

When a bare-root plant is received, unwrap it and soak it in muddy water for at least eight hours before planting. Plant within 24 hours or wrap it in wet burlap (coarse sacking) or newspaper and store in a cool (4°C/40°F), dark place for up to a week. If it cannot be planted after seven days, resoak and heel it in a trench at a 45° angle. Cover completely with several inches of moist soil. Roses can remain entrenched for up to six weeks. However, unless it is too cold, it is best to plant bare-root roses as soon as possible after they arrive.

1 With a spade, dig a hole at least a spade's depth (30–45cm/12–18in) deep and at least 30cm (12in) wide. The hole must be wide enough to accommodate the roots of the plant with several centimetres or inches to spare.

2 Fill the hole with water and let it soak in so that the deeper roots will have moisture. If any water is still standing in the hole after an hour or two, dig deeper, break up the soil, and add sand to increase drainage. In the meantime, amend the soil dug from the hole. Add at least a spadeful of well-rotted manure, peat moss, compost or leaf mould, and a cup of superphosphate and mix well.

3 Examine the bare-root plant. Prune to three or four healthy canes, removing any canes thinner than a pencil.

4 Cut back any roots that are damaged or too long.

5 Once the water has drained from the hole, make a mound of amended soil in the centre of the hole, forming a cone to support the roots. Generally, in areas with winter temperatures below freezing, position the bud union 2.5–5cm (1–2in) below soil level; in milder climates, position the bud union up to 5cm (2in) above soil level.

6 Position the plant so the bud union is at the proper level, and spread the roots down over the cone. Add the amended soil, filling two-thirds of the hole. Add water to the top of the hole and let it soak in.

7 Fill in the rest of the hole with soil, and gently firm by hand. Stepping on the soil to firm causes too much compaction. Add moist soil, covering two-thirds of the plant. This serves as protection from wind and weather, while providing extra moisture so the plant can develop properly.

8 Check the plant at least once a week. When new growth is 2.5–5cm (1–2in) long, gently remove the extra soil, smooth to soil level and mulch well.

Growing roses in containers

Bare-root roses do not do as well in containers as those already growing in cardboard or nursery cans. For a full-sized rose, a container should be at least 45cm (18in) in diameter with a depth of 60cm (24in) to provide enough space for root development. Many types of containers are suitable for roses, from whisky barrels to glazed pottery to plastic pots. Terracotta is attractive, but it is very porous. A benefit is that water evaporates, keeping the plant cool in summer, but as a result the plant dries out faster than in other containers. Do not use any type of metal container for roses. Metal conducts heat well, so the soil gets too warm in summer, eventually killing the plant.

Make sure the container has at least two or three drainage holes in the bottom. Raise the container a little way off the ground so that water can drain out and the plant does not drown, especially in heavy rain. A footed container is ideal, or place the container on bricks or casters, or fashion an 'X' out of lengths of wood and set the container on that.

ABOVE A good organic mulch – such as decayed manure – deters weeds and adds humus to the soil, providing nutrients and improving soil structure.
~

Place a curved pottery shard over the drainage holes to prevent soil from running out of the pot. Add several centimetres or inches of coarse gravel to the bottom of the container. Roses can be grown in good garden soil amended as above, but I prefer to use sterile potting soil or a soil-less mixture purchased at a garden centre. Mix three parts of prepared potting soil or soil-less mix with one part organic matter (compost, well-rotted manure, leaf mould, peat moss). Put several centimetres or inches of the soil mix into the container and set the plant at the proper height. Add soil to near the top of the pot. Gently firm the soil, water well and mulch.

Roses in containers do best in a bright location with at least six hours of sun a day. Water as necessary, but no less than twice a week, more in hot weather, and more if in an unglazed clay container. Keep the plants away from light-coloured walls, as the walls can reflect too much light in the summer. Turn the containers every few days to encourage upright growth, as the plants tend to lean towards the sun.

MULCHING

There are some rosarians who swear by mulch, and others who contend that a rose bed should be left with the soil exposed. I am a firm believer in mulching for several reasons. A good covering of mulch (several centimetres or inches) cuts down on weeds. It also keeps the soil temperature constant, and cuts down on loss of soil moisture through evaporation. As an organic mulch breaks down over time, it adds humus to the soil, provides nutrients and improves soil structure.

When mulching an established bed for the first time, first weed the bed thoroughly. Pull up any unwanted plants, being sure to get the roots; add them to the compost pile. Lightly cultivate (turn over) the top 2 or 3cm (1in) of soil. Cover the entire bed with 5 to 10cm (2 to 4in) of mulch, leaving a 10cm (4in) circle unmulched at the base of each plant.

Organic mulch gradually decomposes. As the lower layer becomes part of the soil, new mulch needs to be added, usually once a year. The material used for mulch is a matter of personal preference. Some mulches give a formal look while some look more natural. Buckwheat hulls, pine needles, wood chips, wood shavings, shredded bark, pine bark nuggets, chopped oak or other leaves, peanut hulls, grass clippings, straw, sawdust, well-rotted manure, hop manure or even ground corn-cobs can be used as mulch. Depending on availability, some of these mulches are free for the asking at timber (lumber) mills or granaries, while others are costly for covering a large area. As these mulches break down, they use up some of the nitrogen in the soil. When using an organic mulch, substitute a higher nitrogen ratio fertilizer for the 5–10–5 recommended in the next section, such as 10–10–10, 15–10–5 or 10–10–5.

Spun polyester fabrics and porous black plastic are man-made mulches. When using either on a new bed, first lay down the mulch, and then cut holes for planting. They can also be cut to fit around established plants. They are unattractive by themselves, and are best covered with a thin layer of shredded bark. These types of man-made mulch dictate the use of a water soluble fertilizer or foliar feed so that the roses can get nutrients.

Recycle old newspapers by using them as a mulch. Spread out a thickness of eight or more sheets, or shred the newspaper. Cover the paper thinly with a more attractive material, such any organic or inorganic mulch, to anchor it in place. Newsprint breaks down over time, and the ink contains micro-nutrients which are beneficial to the soil. Coloured newspaper contains some heavy metals; do not use it in the garden.

ABOVE An automated sprinkler system should only be used early in the day, allowing time for the foliage to dry out before nightfall.
~

FEEDING

Even though roses are heavy feeders, a newly planted rose should not be fertilized for at least a month. Feed species roses, shrub roses, ramblers and climbers only once in early spring, just before they leaf out.

Floribundas, grandifloras and hybrid teas need a minimum of three feedings a year (four in areas with no winter freeze): the first in early spring after the shrub starts to leaf out, the second in late spring or early summer as flowering begins, and the third in late summer to keep the rose going until autumn. The optional fourth feeding in warmer areas is in the autumn. Some rosarians keep to a stricter schedule, feeding every six weeks until late summer, or even as often as once a month.

Types of fertilizers – organic and inorganic

There is much disagreement among rosarians as to what type of fertilizer to use on roses. There are commercial fertilizers specially formulated for roses. Follow package instructions for application rates. Alternatively, apply a granular, general purpose fertilizer with an N–P–K (Nitrogen – Phosphorus (Potash) – Potassium) ratio of 5–10–5 at the rate of one handful (or cupful) per plant.

For a more organic approach to feeding, top-dress with compost or other well-rotted organic material, ½ cup of rock phosphate or bone meal, and ½ cup greensand in early spring. Follow with a liquid foliar (leaf) feed every two to four weeks until August. There are a number of products on the market for foliar feeding, including fish emulsion, kelp or seaweed emulsion. Be sure to dilute them according to package specifications, and do not apply in the heat of the day or on a day when the temperature is above 27°C (80°F), or you risk burning the leaves. Until recently, it was thought that plants got all their nutrition from the soil through their roots. Scientists have now learned that most plants, not just epiphytic orchids and bromeliads, get nutrients through their leaves. Foliar feeding with a suitable product makes the nutrients immediately available to the plant.

A number of newer concepts in feeding can be included in any fertilizing regimen. At the time of the spring feeding, water each plant with 1 tablespoon of Epsom salts diluted in 4.5 litres (1 gallon) of water. The magnesium in the Epsom salts keeps the canes and stems strong. For the last feeding of the season, use a formulation without nitrogen, such as 0–10–10, applied at a rate of ½ cup per rose bush. Nitrogen promotes foliar growth. By autumn, it is more important to have a strong plant with good strong roots, than one with lots of new growth that will die at the first hard frost.

ABOVE Leaky pipe irrigation waters the soil, not the plant leaves, therefore minimizing the risk of fungal diseases.

~

When applying granular fertilizer or other amendment, gently scratch it into the uppermost layer of soil surrounding the rose bush with a hoe or a hand fork. Make sure not to get any on the canes or bud union. Water the plant well after fertilizing.

WATERING

Not only are roses heavy feeders, they also need a lot of water. It is impossible to say that roses must have a certain amount of water, although the equivalent of 2.5cm (1in) of rainfall a week is the absolute minimum. There are many factors to take into account in judging the amount of water a rose needs, the first of which is the weather. In many areas the rainfall provides sufficient water for most of the season. Get an inexpensive rain gauge to accurately measure the rainfall. I have been surprised to find that after what I had thought to be a downpour, but of short duration, the gauge only registered about 1cm (½in) of rain, yet after a day of steady light rain, the gauge showed about 3cm (over an inch) had fallen. If the weather is hot and humid, plants need less water than if it is hot and dry. When it is hot and dry and breezy, plants need the most water, as much moisture is lost through transpiration.

Young or newly transplanted roses need more water than established plants. Roses in containers need more frequent watering than those in the ground, with ones in unglazed pottery needing the most frequent waterings.

To determine if a rose needs watering, stick your middle finger down into the soil. The soil should feel moist to the touch. If it feels dry more than 2 or 3cm (1in) down, water immediately.

When planting roses, some rosarians mound up soil around each bush, effectively creating a dike or catch basin so that all water is directed at the root area. Others do not build individual dikes, but create a large one around the entire bed. In some very cold areas, roses are planted in raised beds with moats dug around them, with two-fold advantages: the soil in raised beds warms earlier than surrounding soil, and the moat catches the rainwater, directing it towards the root area of the plants.

Sprinkling versus irrigating

This is yet another topic of dispute for rosarians. No matter which method is employed, it is important to water deeply and slowly. The soil should be moist at least 30 to 45cm (12 to 18in) deep after watering. To check, dig down to that depth after watering. If the soil is not moist, extend the watering time; if the soil is very moist at 45cm (18in), decrease the watering time. It is almost better not to water than to give plants a light watering. Light watering encourages shallow roots, which are insufficient to anchor or feed the plant. Being close to the soil line, they are easily damaged by cultivation and fertilization.

Most sprinklers and overhead watering systems cover a large area. The water is not directed just to the root areas where it is needed, so it is necessary to keep the water on for a longer period of time to achieve the desired moisture level in the soil than if watering by hand or irrigating. Many older automated systems use sprinklers, but it is costly to change them to irrigation lines. If sprinkling or overhead watering is the choice, do it early in the day so that the leaves dry out thoroughly before the cool and damp of the evening.

There are several different types of slow-drip irrigation systems. A leaky pipe or soaker hose system oozes water along its entire length. Although it provides a slow flow of water with no danger of flooding the soil, the water is not concentrated in the root areas, but goes in between plants. Depending on the configuration, even garden paths get watered. The main advantage is that the leaves do not get wet, so fungal disease is less likely to occur. These hoses can be buried (depending on the climate) under the mulch, so the mulch is not disturbed. Such a system can be automated. Getting even more technologically advanced is a small computerized control which attaches to the water tap (faucet), monitoring rainfall and turning on the irrigation when needed, not during a downpour. Because the hose is underground, there is often no evidence of any leak or break in the system until the plants begin to dry out.

Other irrigation systems have plastic piping either laid on the top of the soil, or slightly buried with emitters strategically

ABOVE **Pruning tools** *(from top to bottom): fine toothed pruning saw;
long-handled cutters; pruning sheers (secateurs).*

placed where needed. The emitters can be of two types: one which slowly drips water underground, or one that comes slightly above ground level and slowly bubbles water.

Hand-watering is the old fashioned way to water, but works well, especially if you do not have a large number of plants. Water is directed exactly where it is needed, and the proper amount is applied. Hand-watering is ideal if roses are surrounded by built-up basins or dikes. Simply flood that area and go on to the next plant.

WEEDING

A weed by definition is an undesirable plant, as a rose could be considered a weed in an onion patch. Anything other than a rose is undesirable in a rose garden, as roses do not tolerate competition from other plants for either water or nutrition. It is easiest to control weeds when they are young, and can easily be pulled by hand, root and all. Applying 5 to 10cm (2 to 4in) of mulch after weeding keeps many new weeds from growing by forming a thick barrier that most plants do not penetrate. Usually all but the hardiest weeds do not sprout under the cover of a mulch.

PRUNING

Pruning is often intimidating to experienced gardeners and novices alike. However, most roses, especially hybrid teas, grandifloras and floribundas, not only benefit from pruning, but would become a jungle of tangled stems with few flowers if they were left unpruned. Pruning is done to cut out diseased or dead

ABOVE *Make a pruning cut at a 45° angle, no more than 1cm (½in)
above an outward facing bud eye.*

wood, to encourage new growth, and to train the plant in a manner in which it gets optimal air circulation, keeping the crown area as open as possible.

It is important to have the proper tools for pruning. Pruning shears or secateurs are used on canes up to 1cm (½in) in diameter. Long-handled loppers are for canes up to 2.5cm (1in) in diameter and a fine-toothed pruning saw is used for any larger cuts. It helps to have a pair of leather or rubber reinforced gardening gloves to protect your hands from the thorns.

The first cut is the hardest to do psychologically. It is important to remember that one cut, even if poorly done, is not going to kill the plant. Take a deep breath, relax and learn how to prune properly. It is quite easy when you know what you are doing. Most pruning cuts are made at a 45° angle. Practice cutting

ABOVE A rose before spring pruning.

~

ABOVE A rose after spring pruning, with all the dead canes removed.

~

on a dead cane, working your way down from the top. As you are cutting, keep a look out for bud eyes. They are small nubs on the stem. During the growing season they are easily found in the crotch between a leaf attachment and a stem. When pruning, it is best to make the cut just above (not more than 1cm or ½in) an outward-facing bud eye. This encourages outward growth. If you do not pay attention to the location of the bud eyes, the plant will soon become unruly. Once you have mastered cutting at a 45° angle to an outward-facing bud eye, you can prune any rose.

To ensure a clean cut, have the cutting blade on the lower side of the cane. The pressure is applied on the non-cutting side so any injury is on the part of the cane that is being cut off. Large cuts can be covered, if wished, with pruning paint.

Floribundas, grandifloras and hybrid tea roses

In the spring, prune out any dead wood, cutting down to healthy, white tissue. Prune to eliminate crossed canes, and any weak or thin canes. A heavy or severe pruning can rejuvenate a vigorous old bush, producing very showy blooms. In this case, prune back all but three or four canes, leaving them at a height of 15 to 30cm (6 to 12in).

In moderate pruning, the best method for most garden roses, leave five to twelve canes 45 to 60cm (18 to 24in) high. This produces a good quantity of blooms on a vigorous shrub. Do a light pruning only on a weak plant, or one over 1.5m (5ft) tall. Use this method on species roses. Cut back one-third the height on all the canes. Light pruning produces a large number of short-stemmed flowers on tall bushes.

In the summer, do not prune one or two-year-old plants except to remove any dead or diseased canes. On older and established plants, cut blossoms (dead or alive) just above a five- or seven-leaflet leaf (never above a three-leaflet leaf), keeping at least two leaves on the cane. Suckers often appear, which are canes coming up from the rootstock. They look different to the rest of the plant and should be removed. The most satisfactory method is to pull the sucker downwards and tear it out from the crown. Cutting it out leaves eyes at the bases from which additional suckers can grow.

In areas with cold winters, stop cutting roses in September and allow the plant to go dormant naturally. Pruning encourages new growth which would not be hardy enough to withstand the winter. Enjoy blossoms in the garden, remove their petals when they have gone past and let them set fruit. In mid to late autumn (fall), any canes over 1.5m (5ft) tall can be cut back so that they do not whip about in the wind, damaging themselves.

Miniatures

Miniature roses should be pruned sparingly. Remove any dead wood or excess growth that is out of proportion to the rest of the plant. Never cut back any more than half the length of a cane. Any other pruning on miniatures is to encourage good shape and branching.

Climbers and ramblers

Do nothing to a climbing rose during its first two years except to remove dead canes or any very twiggy growth. In ensuing years, remove dead wood in the spring, and cut back any very long branches to average length. Cut as close as possible to the main cane. Get an overall view of the climber to see the shape it will take. Prune back all laterals and tie them up. Curve around a trellis or bend along a fence, creating as many horizontals as possible. Pointing the canes down produces the most flowers. In the autumn (fall), remove one old cane for each new cane. After the rose blooms, dead-head, leaving two or three buds.

Ramblers bloom only once, early in the season. This year's new growth will produce next year's flowers. Cut back that which bloomed this year. Remove any suckers that grow up from the understock. Train ramblers by wrapping the canes around arches and pillars and tying in place.

Standards or tree roses

In early spring prune back any dead wood. In summer, cut back to five-leafed leaflets with an outward-facing bud eye. Prune back as necessary to keep good shape and form.

ABOVE *In summer, prune 1cm (½in) above an outward facing five-leaflet leaf to encourage a new stem to grow away from the centre of the plant. Note the new red growth.*

~

PREPARING PLANTS FOR WINTER DORMANCY

It is important to keep rose beds clean of litter and fallen leaves, especially in the autumn, as many diseases can overwinter in the soil. As the days get shorter, refrain from pruning or cutting roses for indoor use. Just before the first frost date, remove any remaining leaves from the roses.

Floribundas, grandifloras and hybrid teas

At the end of the growing season, but before the killing frost (the first heavy frost of the year), mound up 10 to 15cm (4 to 6in) of light soil or compost around established plants. In areas where the temperatures get below −18°C (0°F), gradually make the mound higher, allowing each successive layer to freeze, until a height of 30cm (12in) has been reached. If very cold weather sets in and the soil mound becomes frozen, mulch with leaves or straw. Cover new plants completely as tender canes will be killed by extreme cold.

ABOVE A rose, well mulched and protected through the cold months, breaks winter dormancy in good condition.

~

Standards or tree roses

Roses trained as trees or standards need a more complicated preparation for winter. In areas with moderately cold winters, cut back top canes just before the killing frost. Wrap the truck and top with salt hay. After the winter freeze sets in, cover the entire plant with burlap (coarse sacking). In areas with extremely severe winters it is preferable to bury the entire tree. Do this by gently digging under half of the roots. Bend the bush over to the other side into a trench. Use crossed stakes to hold the trunk in place. Bury the entire plant with a 15cm (6in) covering of soil.

Climbers

Before the killing frost, carefully untie the canes from their supports and arch them down to ground level. Use several crossed stakes to hold the canes in place. Cover with at least 15cm (6in) of soil. Place markers at the crown and at the tops of the canes to indicate where the rose is buried.

When spring arrives, do not rush to remove winter protection. The weather is often very changeable and even a light frost can kill tender growth. Peep under the mulch to see if growth has begun. If danger of frost is past, gently remove the mulch, taking care not to injure the new growth. It is a good idea to keep some salt hay on hand just in case a late freeze threatens. A light covering with salt hay can make the difference between a plant that thrives and one that fails due to late winterkill.

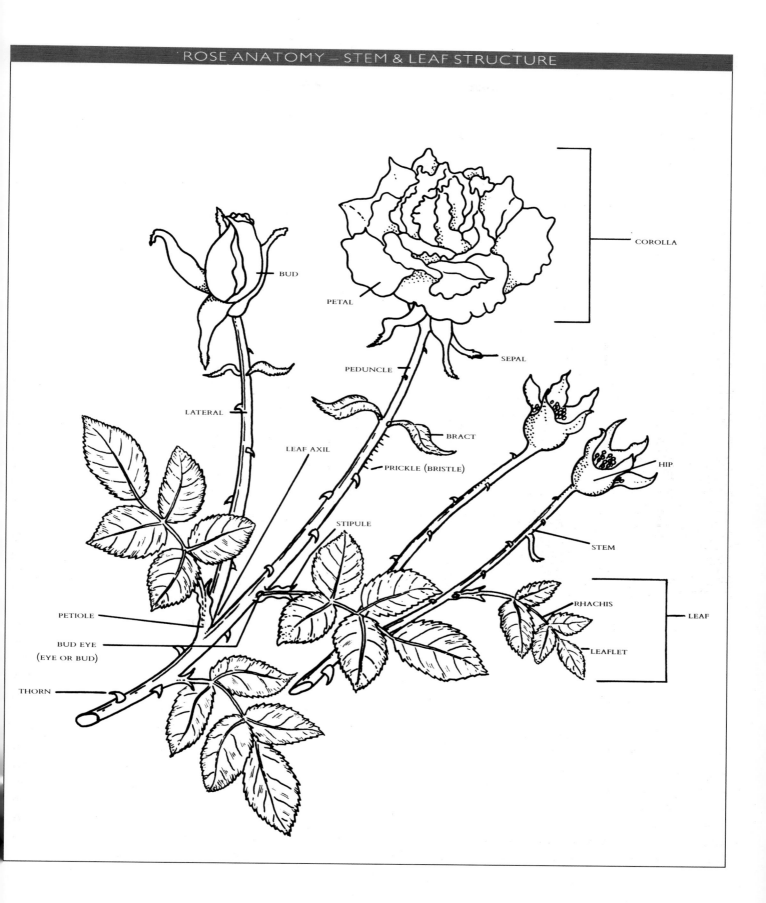

ROSE ANATOMY — STEM & LEAF STRUCTURE

COROLLA

BUD

PETAL

SEPAL

PEDUNCLE

LATERAL

BRACT

LEAF AXIL

PRICKLE (BRISTLE)

HIP

STIPULE

STEM

PETIOLE

RHACHIS

BUD EYE
(EYE OR BUD)

LEAF

LEAFLET

THORN

PESTS, DISEASES AND CONTROL

A vigorous rose is much less likely to succumb to infestation or predation than a weak plant. The first step towards a vigorous rose is to choose a healthy plant from an established nursery or mail-order company. Then follow the steps outlined in the chapter on cultivation. Choose a suitable site with at least six hours of sun a day, good drainage, good air circulation and away from root competition of other trees or shrubs, allowing enough space between plants. Supply ample water and keep the beds clear of weeds and debris.

Some people are hesitant to grow roses because they think that roses demand too much attention. It is true that you cannot simply plant a rose and other than watering it regularly ignore it for the growing season and expect it to perform well. Roses do demand some work and attention, but much of it is preventative.

Examine your plants at least once a week. Look close, go beyond the admiration of your flowers. Any problem caught in the early stages on a single plant is easier to control or eradicate than one that has run rampant throughout the garden.

Special care needs to be taken when cutting off diseased material from any plant. Make sure the blades of the pruners or saw are kept sharp and dip or wipe them in alcohol or bleach after each cut. This keeps the problem from spreading to healthy tissue. Burn, discard or in some manner destroy any infested or diseased material removed from your plants. Do not compost it or shred it for mulch, as that will spread the problem to the rest of the garden.

Be certain of your diagnosis before you begin any treatment programme whether it is organic or involves the use of a synthetic chemical. Do not assume that a wilted cane has been attacked by borers; first review your basic gardening practices. Has the plant received at least 2.5cm (1in) of water each week? Has the temperature been over 32°C (90°F)? See if a good drink of water reverses the condition. When the weather is very hot a plant needs more water than it does at cooler temperatures.

Yellowing of leaves may not necessarily indicate a lack of iron, but may be due to an alkaline soil. If you followed the recommendations for planting, there should not be a pH problem. If it is an older established plant, check the soil pH. There are kits available, or you can take a soil sample to a garden centre for

LEFT Every rose gardener strives toward producing healthy and pest-free specimens such as this delightful 'White Delight' rose. This chapter will help you to avoid, identify and treat the pests and diseases that most commonly affect roses.
~

ABOVE *When removing diseased material, dip the blades of your pruning tools in alcohol or bleach after each cut to prevent the spread of disease to healthy tissue.*
~

Pay special attention to directions for dilution and application. Wear protective clothing, rubber gloves and mask if indicated. Spraying should be carried out on a still day so there is no danger of the chemical drifting onto other plants. Apply early in the morning or in the evening to avoid harming bees and other beneficial insects.

PESTS

Aphids

SYMPTOMS – The flowers and leaves may appear stunted or deformed. Look for clusters of small (less than 3mm or ⅛in), soft-bodied insects which may be brown, green (greenfly) or reddish in colour. Generally found on the undersides of leaves, on buds or new growth, aphids are sucking insects that feed on the plant's juices. Another sign of aphids is a sweet, sticky substance (honeydew) on the plant that attracts ants.

TREATMENT – Treat with insecticidal soap, pyrethrum, rotenone (derris), pirimicarb-methyl or malathion. Ladybirds (ladybugs) are a natural enemy of aphids and can keep them controlled if introduced into the garden.

ABOVE *Aphids are very small insects usually found on buds or new growth. They feed on the plant's juices, leading to stunted or deformed growth in the flowers and leaves.*
~

it to be tested. Alkaline soil can be adjusted to roses' preferred pH of 6.0 to 6.5 by adding aluminium sulphate to the soil at the recommended rate.

The following pages list many of the pests and diseases that can affect roses. For each problem, the symptom section includes the obvious signs of the problem, the diagnosis and description of the causative agent. The treatment section first mentions any preventative measures which can be taken to avoid the problem (if any are available). Secondly, it describes non-toxic controls including pruning, hand-picking insects, natural predators (beneficial nematodes, lacewings, ladybirds [ladybugs]), natural insecticides (pyrethrum, rotenone [derris]) and soaps. Natural controls are available, such as B.t. *(Bacillus thurengiensis)* which is sold as a powder and milky spore disease *(Bacillus popilliae)* in the United States. The last to be listed are the synthetic chemicals (benomyl, carbaryl, pirimicarb-methyl and malathion). When using any control, read and follow all label directions carefully.

Beetles

SYMPTOMS – Beetles chew holes in the leaves and can often be found inside the flower petals, chewing their way out. There are a number of beetles, which include chafers, that attack roses.

TREATMENT – Hand-pick the beetles or gently shake the bush over a cloth or paper. Depending on your inclination, they can be destroyed in any number of ways: the simplest method is to step on them firmly. When in the larval or grub stage, beetles can eat plant roots. In the United States, milky spore disease *(Bacillus propilliae)* kills the grub stage. Once applied to cultivated ground or lawn, it may take several years to establish itself, but milky spore remains in the soil for up to 30 years, killing off grubs as they develop. Alternatively apply pyrethrum, rotenone (derris), carbaryl or malathion.

ABOVE *Skeletonized leaves are another sign of caterpillar damage.*

~

ABOVE *Beetles can cause serious damage, eating their way through leaves and flowers.*

~

Borers

SYMPTOMS – A number of insects bore into the canes and stems of roses where they lay their eggs. As the larvae develop, they eat the cane or stem causing sudden wilting of any area above the infestation.

TREATMENT – Simply cut off and destroy the damaged stem or cane, taking care to cut at least 2.5cm (1in) below the wilted area so as to remove the larvae. Cut as when pruning – at a 45° angle 0.5cm (¼in) above an outward-facing bud.

Caterpillars

SYMPTOMS – The larval stages of a number of butterflies and moths feed on rose leaves and flowers with damage ranging from small holes to skeletonized leaves. Some, known as leafrollers, curl or roll the leaves around themselves for protection while eating their way out.

TREATMENT – Pick off by hand and destroy. For leafrollers, simply unroll the leaf and remove the caterpillar or pick off the affected leaves and destroy. Alternatively, caterpillars can be controlled with B.t., derris, pyrethrum, pirimiphos-methyl, malathion or carbaryl.

Leafhoppers

SYMPTOMS – Look for pale leaves with small yellow or white spots. With severe infestation, leaves will drop. The 0.5cm (¼in) greenish-yellow insects hop about on the undersides of leaves, sucking out the plant's juices.

TREATMENT – Spray with insecticidal soap, pyrethrum, rotenone (derris) or malathion.

Rose gall

SYMPTOMS – A mossy-looking swelling (up to 7.5cm or 3in diameter) on the stem or cane is caused by larvae of wasp-like insects. Some galls have a pleasant scent, and in Victorian times they were cut from the plant, the larvae removed, and used as sachets to freshen ladies' drawers. Galls occur frequently on the Sweet Briar rose *(Rosa eglanteria).*

TREATMENT – The galls can be pruned out and destroyed, although they cause little harm to the bush.

ABOVE Rosa eglanteria, Sweet Briar Rose, is especially susceptible to the, usually harmless, moss-like swelling known as rose gall.

~

Rose midge

SYMPTOMS – The tell-tale sign of midges is a crook in the stem, usually just below a bud or flower, making the flower bud droop. Leaves and blooms can also blacken and shrivel up. Midges are too small to see with the naked eye; microscopically they look like yellowish-brown or red flies or white maggots.

TREATMENT – Cut off and destroy any infested parts at least 2.5cm (1in) below the problem area.

Rose scale

SYMPTOMS – The foliage turns dark and wilts, dropping prematurely. On older canes, look for small tan, grey or brown hard-shelled, sucking insects that do not move.

TREATMENT – Prune out and destroy affected parts. Spray with dormant oil or tar oil in winter or early spring before buds break dormancy (this is rather a messy treatment and care must be taken not to damage other plants) or use a systemic insecticide.

Spider mite

SYMPTOMS – Initially the leaves have yellowish mottling. Heavier infestation turns leaves from yellow to brown. Leaves then dry, curl up, and eventually fall off. In advanced stages, you can see fine webs on the leaves. If the diagnosis is questionable, cut a suspicious stem and shake it over a sheet of white paper. If dark spots move on the paper, spider mites are confirmed. Microscopically, they look like tiny brown, green-red or yellow spiders.

TREATMENT – Mites can be eliminated by a strong stream of water aimed at both the tops and bottoms of all leaves – repeat for three consecutive days. Spray with insecticidal soap, dust with sulphur, or spray with dimethoate or malathion. Whatever the method, it is important to treat both sides of the leaves.

ABOVE Yellowing leaves can be the first sign of spider mite infestation.

~

DISEASE-RESISTANT ROSES

The following roses are generally resistant to disease. If blackspot and/or mildew is a particular problem in your area, refer to the relevant charts in the A-Z section of the book for roses that are resistant to these diseases.

'Aquarius' (Gr)	'Peace' (HT)
'Bonica' (S)	'Pink Parfait' (Gr)
'Carousel' (Gr)	'Pristine' (HT)
'Cathedral' (F)	'Prominent' ('Korp') (Gr)
'Chicago Peace' (HT)	'Queen Elizabeth' (Gr)
'Confidence' (HT)	'Razzle Dazzle' (F)
'Europeana' (F)	'Rose Parade' (F)
'Evening Star' (F)	'Shreveport' (Gr)
'Fragrant Cloud' (HT)	'Sonia' ('Sweet Promise') (Gr)
'Mister Lincoln' (HT)	'Tiffany' (HT)
'Pascali' (HT)	'Tropicana' ('Super Star') (HT)

KEY: F – FLORIBUNDA GR – GRANDIFLORA
HT – HYBRID TEA S – SHRUB

ABOVE Lacewings are a natural predator of thrips.
~

Thrips

SYMPTOMS – These tiny black, brown or yellow insects are usually a minor problem during the first flush of bloom. They cause deformed flowers, browned edges to petals, or flowers that do not open.

TREATMENT – Remove and destroy affected flowers. Use insecticidal soap, pyrethrum, rotenone (derris) or malathion. Natural predators include certain nematodes, lacewings, ladybirds (ladybugs) and some mites.

DISEASES

Blackspot

SYMPTOMS – This fungal disease first appears as small black spots on leaves. The leaves turn yellow and eventually drop. Blackspot thrives in moist conditions. As droplets of water (rain or overhead watering) fall on infected leaves, spores are released, spreading the disease upwards. The fungus overwinters on the plant on small cane lesions and also on leaves left on the ground. Yellow roses are most susceptible.

TREATMENT – Water plants early in the day. To keep moisture off leaves, water at ground level, using a drip irrigation system. Practise good hygiene in the garden. Immediately remove and destroy any infected leaves or stems. Collect and destroy fallen leaves regularly. Allow for ample room between plants and among stems and canes for good air circulation. Controls include fungicidal soap, sulphur or benomyl applied every two or three

ABOVE The first sign of blackspot; the leaves will eventually turn yellow and drop.
~

weeks. Recent studies show that an application of 2 teaspoonsful of sodium bicarbonate mixed in 4.5 litres (1 gallon) of water with several drops of a mild washing up liquid every four or five days can control fungal diseases. If blackspot is a problem, plant resistant varieties, otherwise regular spraying will be necessary.

Botrytis

SYMPTOMS – Also known as grey mould as the fungus that appears on buds and partially opened flowers is grey-brown. It can also attack young shoots damaged by frost. Pink and white hybrid teas are the most susceptible.

TREATMENT – Pick and destroy infected buds and flowers. Apply fungicidal soap or sulphur. Prune carefully to avoid congestion of growth so that air can circulate freely.

Canker

SYMPTOMS – Brownish lesions appear on the woody tissue of a cane, with poor to no growth above the lesion. This parasitic fungus enters the plant through wounds or weak tissue.

TREATMENT – Good hygiene in the garden can prevent canker. Prune out and destroy affected canes. Make sure to prune back to healthy wood; at least 2.5cm (1in) below the obvious canker. If wished, apply pruning paint to seal the pruning wound.

ABOVE Crown gall is a bumpy, brown, tumour-like growth usually found on the crown of the rose and occasionally the roots.

~

Crown gall

SYMPTOMS – Bumpy, brown, tumour-like growths are found near the crown or sometimes on the roots. The plant appears weak, flowers and foliage become deformed, and the plant can die. Crown gall is caused by a soil-borne bacteria.

TREATMENT – Remove and destroy the plant. Remove soil from the immediate area around the plant. When buying plants, check the crown area to make sure they do not have this problem. Plant new roses in fresh soil well away from the infected area.

Powdery mildew

SYMPTOMS – Leaves, new growth and buds appear greyish or dusted with white powder. New leaves may be deformed. Powdery mildew is a problem when warm days are followed by cool nights.

TREATMENT – Make sure plants are well spaced and well pruned for optimal air circulation. Cut off and destroy affected parts. Treat with fungicidal soap, sulphur or benomyl as needed.

Rust

SYMPTOMS – This first appears as rusty-looking spots on the undersides of leaves. As the infection progresses, yellow blotching appears on the surface of the leaves, finally resulting in defoliation.

TREATMENT – Prune out all affected parts of the plant. Use fungicidal soap, sulphur as needed.

ABOVE Greyish leaves indicate powdery mildew.

~

Virus

SYMPTOMS – Yellow streaking or mottling on leaves often appears early in the season.

TREATMENT – In some countries virus may disappear by itself as the season progresses and affected leaves can be pruned out for aesthetic reasons. Elsewhere the plant may lose all its leaves and eventually die. If virus is suspected it is best to dig up and destroy the plant. New roses should be purchased from a reputable source and planted in fresh soil away from the affected site. There is no suitable chemical treatment.

OTHER ROSE PROBLEMS

Balling

SYMPTOMS – Flowers do not open fully. Buds swell during good weather, but during a long period of wet, cool weather the outside petals rot, encapsulating the inner ones.

TREATMENT – Cut off affected flowers to prevent possible infection.

Chlorosis

SYMPTOMS – The leaf appears anaemic, with an all-over yellowish tinge. This is a mineral deficiency, due to a lack of iron. Yellow and orange-flowered roses and *Rosa rugosa* are most susceptible.

TREATMENT – Spray with chelated iron and water deeply.

LEFT A viral infection is indicated by yellow streaking or stippling on the leaves, appearing early in the season.
BELOW In wet, cool weather the outer petals of a flower may rot, encapsulating the inner ones to form a ball shape – a condition known as balling.
~

PROPAGATING AND HYBRIDIZING ROSES

Some people are not content to merely grow great roses, they want to create them as well. It is not too difficult to replicate an existing rose plant. There are several methods of propagation, all of which require more patience than skill. Creating a brand new rose takes even more patience, but the techniques are not complicated. Meticulous attention to detail is the key to successful hybridization.

Be aware that many modern roses are patented. This means that they cannot be propagated without permission and without paying royalties to the patent owner. The legalities are less clear about using a patented rose for hybridization, but it is best to avoid any future problem by using non-patented roses for garden experimentation. All patented roses must have a metal tag attached which identifies the plant and its patent number.

PROPAGATING

There are three methods of reproducing roses: from cuttings, by layering and by budding. Propagating roses from cuttings is the simplest method, and budding is the most complex. Using either the layering or cutting technique produces own-root plants. Budding is a grafting technique, producing roses like those in the market-place which have one type of rose that produces the flowers grafted onto another that is good rootstock.

OPPOSITE Most of the beautiful roses available today are the result of successive hybridization.
~

LEFT In 1867, 'La France' a cross between a hybrid perpetual and a tea rose, became the first of a new class of rose, the hybrid tea, so named in recognition of the parentage.
~

PROPAGATING FROM CUTTINGS

This method of propagation works well with shrub roses, old roses, hybrid teas and floribundas and should be carried out in late spring. The best medium for rooting rose cuttings is a mixture of equal parts of moistened soil, peat moss, and sand, vermiculite or perlite. Remember, the chances are that at least one cutting will root, so don't be discouraged if one or more die in the process. To prevent confusion, do not mix cuttings from different roses in the same pot.

1 Cut the faded flower by cutting 15–20cm (6–8in) below the bloom, just above a five- or seven-leaflet leaf.

2 Cut off the top 5cm (2in) just above a leaf. Remove all but the top two sets of leaves, being careful not to damage the bud eyes.

3 Dip the bottom two or three centimetres (inch) of the cutting into rooting hormone, and the cutting is ready to plant.

4 Place a curved pot shard over the drainage hole of a 15cm (6in) pot. Add soil mix and gently firm. With a pencil, make four equidistant 9cm (3½in) deep holes in the soil. Place a cutting into each hole, and gently firm the soil around each one.

5 Insert three stakes into the soil so they protrude several centimetres or inches above the tops of the cuttings. Place the pot into a large plastic bag and close tightly, creating a greenhouse environment.

Store the pot in a shady spot, away from bright sunlight. If the covered pot is exposed to sunlight, the greenhouse effect causes temperatures inside the bag too high for the cuttings to survive.

Be patient. Do not open the bag or disturb the pot for at least eight weeks. If any of the cuttings turn brown or black, they have died. As long as the leaves and stem remain green, the cutting is alive. Observe the beginning of new growth on the stem. Once new growth is well established, remove the bag, and gently pot each rooted cutting in its own pot. If all four root, repot the entire group as a unit. Place the repotted cuttings in a partially shaded spot in the garden for two to three weeks. Then remove the cutting or cuttings from the pot and plant in the rose garden. Mound all of each plant with soil as the weather begins to get cold. In spring, remove the protective soil and enjoy your first propagated roses.

LAYERING

This alternative method of propagation should also be carried out in late spring.

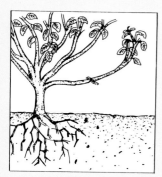

1 Select a low-growing cane, and gently bend it towards the soil. Make a cut half-way through the cane on the underside of the area where the cane touches the soil. Insert a matchstick into the cut to keep it open.

2 Remove the soil from an area 15cm (6in) long, 7.5cm (3in) wide and 15cm (6in) deep where the cut cane touches the soil. Refill with a mixture of equal parts of moistened soil, peat moss, and sand, perlite or vermiculite.

3 Centre the cut and bury a 10cm (4in) length of the cane, covering with 2.5cm (1in) of soil. Cover with a brick. Brace the tip end of the cane so that it can continue to grow upward; this will become the main cane of the new plant. The cut area will soon begin to develop roots. Mulch the growing end as winter approaches.

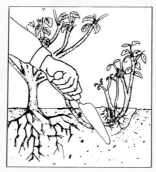

4 In spring, sever the rooted portion from the parent rose. Dig it up, keeping the root ball intact, and plant in the garden.

BUDDING

Propagation by budding or bud-grafting yields a consistently vigorous and hardy root system. *Rosa multiflora* and the climbing 'Dr Huey' are the most commonly used rootstocks. In the autumn root 20 to 25cm (8 to 10in) cuttings of the rootstock, leaving the top two buds to develop. The following summer, cut several 10 to 13cm (4 to 5in) pieces of mature wood from the rose you want to propagate. The wood is properly mature when thorns break off cleanly with little effort, showing green wood underneath. Remove all the thorns from the wood and cut off the leaves, leaving a centimetre (½in) stub of the leaf stem. Wrap in plastic and refrigerate for several weeks.

1 Cut a scion (a bud with a small portion of surrounding tissue) from the budwood that is 2cm (¾in) long and 0.5cm (¼in) wide and deep.

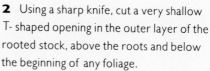

2 Using a sharp knife, cut a very shallow T-shaped opening in the outer layer of the rooted stock, above the roots and below the beginning of any foliage.

3 Insert the scion into the cut, making sure that the bud goes all the way into the cut. Press the cut T onto the scion.

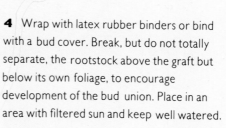

4 Wrap with latex rubber binders or bind with a bud cover. Break, but do not totally separate, the rootstock above the graft but below its own foliage, to encourage development of the bud union. Place in an area with filtered sun and keep well watered.

The following spring, if the bud takes, healthy foliage will emerge from the graft site. Only then can the rootstock foliage be completely severed. Plant in the garden as you would a container-grown rose.

HYBRIDIZING

The greatest challenge and thrill to any rose grower is to create a new rose. Most of today's roses are themselves hybrids that have been created by crossing and recrossing successive generations of roses. Hybridizing is not difficult, but the steps must be followed exactly. If you create a truly new and unique rose, you may find a grower who is willing to test it. With luck and patience, a new rose developed from a cross made this year could find its way into the market-place in ten years.

Choose the roses that you want to breed. It does not make a difference which acts as the male or which acts as the female. Hybridizers often make several crosses between the same two roses, merely reversing their roles. Find partially opened buds of each rose and carefully remove the petals from both. The reproductive organs are now visible. The stamens (or male parts) surround the pistils (or female parts). The ends of the stamens that bear the pollen are called anthers. With a sharp knife remove the anthers from both flowers, taking care not to damage the pistils. Put the anthers from the male rose in a covered tin or jar and set it aside to dry. Discard the anthers from the female rose; they are removed so that the rose does not self-pollinate. Cover the female with a paper bag to prevent pollination from another rose.

Within a day or two, the anthers ripen and release their pollen. At the same time, the female stigma becomes sticky. With a fine brush, transfer the pollen to the stigma. Label the pollinated rose and cover with a bag to protect it from unwanted pollen and other particles.

If the pollination takes, the fruit or hip remains green and within several weeks it swells. If the hip dries up and falls off the plant, do not be discouraged. Although the pollination was not successful, try again. The success rate even among professionals is low. In two to three months the hip ripens and changes colour (bright red, yellow, orange or brown depending on the rose). Pick the hips when the colour changes; overripe seeds do not germinate well. Carefully cut the hip and remove the seeds. There can be any number of seeds within the hip. Stratify (cold condition) the seeds in a plastic bag with peat moss at 4°C (40°F) for six weeks.

Fill a shallow tray (with drainage holes) with fine sand or vermiculite. Remove the shell coat from the seeds and plant between 1 and 2cm (about ½in) deep. Water well. Keep warm (13 to 16°C, 55 to 60°F) and moist, but not soggy, in a dark place until the seeds germinate. Move them into a lighted area, providing 16 hours of light a day. When the first set of true leaves emerges, transplant into a seed bay filled with a mixture of equal parts sterilized topsoil, perlite and peat moss. When making this mixture in quantity, add 1 cup dolomite lime, 1 cup rose food, and 1 cup superphosphate per 35 litres (1 bushel) of soil mix. Continue to give the seedlings 16 hours of light and keep them at 21°C (70°F). Seedlings can bloom as young as seven weeks. That is the time to decide whether to continue the hybridization experiment or to start again with different parents.

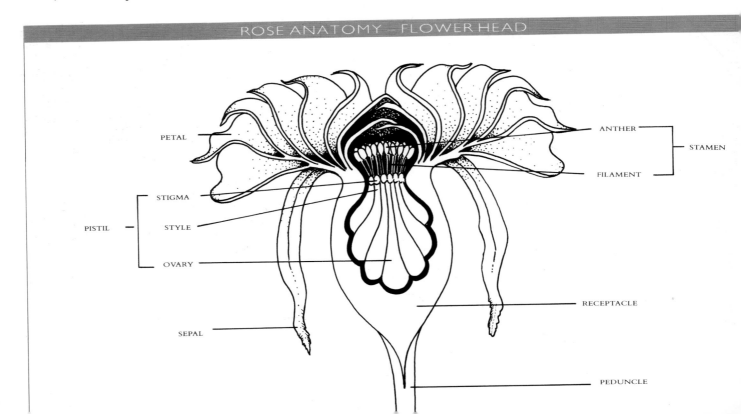

ROSE ANATOMY – FLOWER HEAD

PETAL

ANTHER

STAMEN

FILAMENT

STIGMA

PISTIL

STYLE

OVARY

RECEPTACLE

SEPAL

PEDUNCLE

1 Select the two roses you wish to breed. Remove the petals of a partially opened bud from each rose to expose the reproductive organs.

2 Remove the anthers from both flowers with a sharp knife; do not damage the pistils. Cover the female flower .

3 Put the anthers from the male rose in a covered tin and set aside to ripen – this will occur in about two days.

4 Using a small brush, transfer the pollen released by the ripened male anthers to the sticky female stigma.

5 Label and cover the pollinated rose with a bag to protect it from contamination.

6 Successful pollination results in a healthy green hip that will swell within several weeks.

BEYOND THE GARDEN

There is great satisfaction in growing roses, and the joy need not end in the garden. You can cut roses from the garden to enjoy in bouquets and arrangements indoors, extending the enjoyment up to a week or so. An added challenge to rose growing is to grow for exhibition. There are techniques in addition to cutting and conditioning that help to produce a show-quality rose. Rose-buds and petals can be dried for making pot-pourri and for use in dried flower arrangements. Their beauty and fragrance can last for months. Rose petals and hips are edible, adding gustatory pleasure to the long list of rose attributes. Roses can be enjoyed all year round in the home as well as during their blooming season in the garden.

In reviewing the attributes of roses, consider a rose's appeal to the five senses. Although a petal can be soft and sensual, thorns are not alluring to the sense of touch. A rose's beauty is certainly appealing to the sense of sight, while its perfume is enticing to the sense of smell, and the flavour of the petals and hips are appealing to the sense of taste. As for the sense of hearing, there is definitely a contented sigh that comes from a person smelling an especially fragrant rose. Roses are truly sensory delights.

ROSES AS CUT FLOWERS

In late spring and summer when roses are in profusion in the garden, it is always a pleasure to have some of the roses to enjoy in the home. A single rose in a bud vase is a lovely touch anywhere. Use a variety of different roses in arrangements, or combine them with other flowers. An arrangement can be simple or formal, traditional or avant-garde. Enjoy the creation.

People often complain that cut roses do not last long. When cut and treated properly, a rose can last a week or more; a bud lasts longer than a fully open rose. Combine roses in all stages of maturity for the most natural effect in a bouquet.

Cutting roses

Cut roses early in the morning before the flowers totally open. Remember that cutting a flower is a form of pruning, so follow pruning guidelines. Cut above a five- or seven-leaflet leaf with an outward-facing bud eye at a 45° angle. Immediately put the cut rose into a bucket of water. Work in the shade as much as possible, keeping the bucket of roses out of direct sunlight.

OPPOSITE Roses – displayed in a fresh or dried flower arrangement, an ingredient in pungently scented pot-pourri, or in delicious rose petal butter – essentially appeal to all the senses.
~

BEST ROSES FOR CUTTING

These roses are relatively long-lasting as cut flowers. The ideal cut rose is long-stemmed, so this list is limited to grandifloras (floribundas 'hybrid-tea type') and hybrid teas.

'Aquarius'	'Ole'
'Arizona'	'Olympiad'
'Camelot'	'Paradise'
'Charlotte Armstrong'	'Pascali'
'Chicago Peace'	'Peace'
'Christian Dior'	'Perfume Delight'
'Chrysler Imperial'	'Pristine'
'Double Delight'	'Prominent' ('Korp')
'Duet'	'Queen Elizabeth'
'Electron' ('Mullard Jubilee')	'Royal Highness'
'First Prize'	'Sonia' ('Sweet Promise')
'Fragrant Cloud'	'Swarthmore'
'Garden Party'	'Tiffany'
'Gold Medal'	'Touch of Class'
'Granada'	'Tropicana' ('Super Star')
'Honor'	'White Lightnin''
'Love'	'White Masterpiece'
'Miss All-American Beauty'	'Voodoo'

ABOVE An arrangement of varied hued roses, in bud and in full bloom, graces any setting.
LEFT When gathering roses for flower arrangements, use the pruning technique, that is, cut the stem just above a five- or seven-leaflet leaf with an outward facing bud eye.
~

Conditioning the roses

Once all the roses are cut, bring them to the kitchen or other area with access to a sink and a table or work top. Re-cut each rose under water at a sharp angle at least 0.5cm (¼in) above the end of the stem. Have the vase you will be using nearby for reference. Gently remove all leaves and thorns that will be below the water line when the rose is in the vase. Removing the leaves and thorns opens the stem for good moisture retention underwater, but leads to greater moisture loss in the air, so do not remove ones that will be above the water line.

Immerse the stems in a deep container filled with warm (about 45°C or 110°F) water. When the water cools, put the container in the refrigerator for several hours. This conditioning can revive wilted roses and florist roses.

Adding longer life to an arrangement

To make the flower arrangement, fill a vase with fresh water and add floral preservative (available at florists and garden centres) according to the package directions. A home-made substitute for floral preservative in water is a solution of equal parts of lemonade (soda) and water with ½ teaspoon of bleach added per litre (quart) of solution. Give each rose one final slanted cut before placing it in the arrangement.

For longest life, keep the arrangement out of full sun and in a cool location. Refrigerate at night. Change the water and re-cut the roses every day; add new preservative or use fresh solution.

ABOVE *Rose shows are educational as well as an arena for friendly competition.*
BELOW *This specimen of 'Pristine' is of perfect show quality.*
~

ROSES FOR SHOW

For some rose growers, the challenge of competition is keen, and rose shows are the place for horticultural competition. It takes a lot of work to produce a rose of exhibition quality, but showing a rose you can be proud of makes it all worthwhile.

Rose shows are not all competition, they are educational as well, both for the entrants and the visiting public. It is important to know what you are growing. A rose cannot be entered in competition without its proper name. If you inherited a rose garden (moved into a house with an existing garden) with un-identified plants, invite a knowledgeable rosarian to look at the garden and help identify the plants when they are in bloom.

Roses are judged on a points system, with a set maximum number of points allotted to each prescribed category. The categories and the number of points allotted varies from location to location, but in general the judges will be looking for the following:

- FORM – shape and symmetry in the bloom
- SUBSTANCE – firm, fresh petals
- COLOUR – bright, clear and typical of the particular variety
- STEM – strong and in proportion to the size of the flower
- FOLIAGE – healthy and free from spots caused by water, spraying or disease
- SIZE OF BLOOM – a good size for the variety; generally size is not considered as important as other characteristics
- PRESENTATION – another minor category, but the judges will be looking for an artistic and graceful arrangement

Preparing for the show – in the garden

The stage is set for showing roses in the early spring at the time of pruning. A hard pruning produces fewer canes with larger roses. When the bush sets buds, all secondary buds should be removed. The presence of a side bud on a tea, hybrid tea, or hybrid perpetual rose automatically disqualifies the rose from most competitions.

Choosing the exhibition rose

In choosing a rose for exhibition keep in mind that the roses are judged according to how close to perfection they are for that particular variety. The bloom should be half to three-quarters open, those open less than half do not qualify as blooms. Experiment before the show, cutting roses and storing them to the point of readiness to find out how many days in advance different varieties should be cut. Be prepared for any eventuality. Pick several roses three or four days in advance, in case sudden inclement weather should ruin the roses in the garden.

ABOVE 'Queen Elizabeth' – a grandiflora rose much lauded by rose societies – wins a top award at a local rose show.

~

Grooming

As an animal is groomed before it is entered into competition, so is a rose. Gently rub leaves with a soft dry cloth to make them glossy; use of oil is not allowed. If an outer petal is discoloured or damaged it can be removed so long as it is done without destroying symmetry and no traces of removal are left. A camel's hair brush works wonders for removing small specks of dirt or dust. Blow gently on the centre of a rose to coax it to open a bit more. To transport roses to the competition, wrap each in waxed paper, extending the paper beyond the bloom as protection. It is ideal to carry each rose in a separate container, such as a 1 or 2 litre (quart or half-gallon) drink carton.

The show

Once at the competition, check the blooms one last time, fill out entry forms and place the roses where directed. Then go out and take a long stroll in a garden (someone else's) or go and have a cup of tea. The show is normally closed during judging; entrants have to wait until the show is open to the public to see how they fare. If you do not win an award, do not be discouraged. Read the judges' comments on the entry form (if available) and look at those that did win. It is a good learning experience. Talk to those who enter the same roses and find out what they have done differently. If you win, congratulations. Above all, a rose show should be good-natured fun, a break from the garden, and a chance for an exchange with other people with similar interests.

DRIED ROSES

It is lovely to be able to enjoy some of the beauty and fragrance of roses long after their growing season is past. One way is to have dried roses, either in bouquets, arrangements or pot-pourri.

Air drying

Cut roses (buds or partially opened flowers) early in the day after the dew has dried. Wipe off any moisture and dirt. Remove the lower leaves. Tie the stems with twine and hang the roses upside-down in a warm, dry, dark room. Air drying is easy to do, but the rose colour soon fades from the blooms.

ABOVE When air drying roses, tie the stems with twine and hang, upside-down, in a warm, dry, dark room. Try tying the stems to a coat hanger, which can then be hooked over a peg or nail.

~

DESSICANT DRYING

A dessicant is a fine-grained, moisture absorbing substance. Roses dried in a dessicant do not lose as much colour as those that are air dried. Deep-coloured roses tend to darken while pinks and yellows fade somewhat. Dessicants are now marketed specifically for drying flowers and are available at garden centres, but can be pricey. Several household products work equally well: borax powder, builder's sand that is put in a low-temperature oven (120°C, 250°F) for several hours to remove any moisture (or use beach sand; wash well in a large pail with detergent water, rinse very well three or four times), ground silica gel crystals, or a mixture of equal parts of borax powder and cornflour (cornmeal).

1 The stems of roses do not dry well in dessicants, so remove the stem.

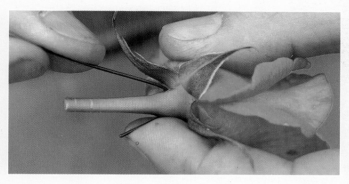

2 Insert a 5-cm (2-in) length of florist's wire about 1cm (½in) into the stem end of the flower. Bend the wire so it is at a 90° angle to the stem.

3 Place the rose into a container filled to one-third with dessicant, and gently pour dessicant between all the petals, completely covering the rose.

4 Space roses about 2.5cm (1in) apart. Cover the container and label with the date. Keep the container in a warm dry area.

If using borax or silica gel, the flowers will dry within several days, while those in sand may take several weeks. Roses can be removed when they rustle and feel dry to the touch, when they should be stored in a dry room until ready to use.

Most dried bouquets and arrangements are best displayed in the winter when the heat is on, keeping the house warm and dry. If the spring and summer are humid, store dried flowers in a warm, dry space.

Pot-pourri

The word 'pot-pourri' comes from the French for medley or stew. It is now taken to mean a mixture of dried flower petals with spices, kept in a jar for its fragrance. The combinations of flowers and spices are only limited by availability and the imagination. Recipes for pot-pourri can be complex or very simple. Use no more than four or five different flowers and leaves and two or three spices. Lavender combines especially well with roses. Other plant material, such as everlasting flowers, cones and evergreen needles, can be added for texture and colour.

Orris root, with its light violet scent, is a commonly used fixative. Gum resins, such as gum arabic, gum styrax, gum benzoin, myrrh or frankincense, can be added to meld the scents of the mixture. The addition of essential oil increases the scent, making the pot-pourri last longer.

Pick roses early in the day. Air dry small rose-buds. Gently remove the petals from opened roses and place them on a screen, cheesecloth or tray in a warm dry place. Collect and dry the other flowers and leaves to be added to the mixture. When using herbs, they are best dried by tying in bundles and hanging upside-down. Label and store each in a screw-top glass jar in a dark place.

Pot-pourri is attractive in any clear container. The fragrance lasts longer if the pot-pourri is not exposed to the air. Some glass pot-pourri containers have decorative metal tops with small holes that allow some of the fragrance to perfume the room. Pot-pourri in an open bowl can be placed in the guest room as an extra welcoming touch.

Dry pot-pourri

■ Gather and dry a selection of rose petals, buds and other flowers and herbs (*see* above).

■ Add 10 to 20 drops of essential oil (rose oil is best in rose pot-pourri, but lavender or vetiver work well) to 4 tablespoons of ground orris root. Put in a tightly closed glass jar for two days.

■ Combine the dried flower petals in a large ceramic, metal, or earthenware bowl. Use 2 cups of rose petals and up to 1 cup each of two other flowers.

■ Add 2 tablespoons of crushed spices, 1½ teaspoonsful of powdered gum resin and ¼ cup dried orange peel (optional).

■ Toss gently, adding the oil-fixative mixture, pour into a 4 litre (gallon) sized glass jar, and seal the cap tightly. Put the jar in a warm, dark place.

■ Gently shake the jar to remix the ingredients every two days. After a month, the pot-pourri should be ready.

POT-POURRI INGREDIENTS

Here is just a selection of possible pot-pourri ingredients. Choose no more than four or five different flowers and leaves, and two or three species, adding everlasting flowers for colour and interest.

FLOWERS

Anise hyssop
Carnation
Chamomile
Heliotrope
Honeysuckle
Jasmine
Lavender
Lemon
Lilac
Lime
Linden
Mignonette
Mock orange
Orange
Pinks
Stock
Sweet pea
Tuberose
Wallflower

HERBS

Angelica
Basil*
Bay leaves
Costmary
Hyssop*
Lemon balm*
Lemon basil*
Lemon grass
Lemon thyme*
Lemon verbena*
Marjoram*
Peppermint*
Rosemary*
Scented geranium*
(all varieties)
Spearmint*
Summer savoury*
Tarragon
Thyme

Flowers can be used in addition to leaves

SPICES

Allspice
Anise
Caraway
Cardamom
Cinnamon
Cloves
Coriander
Cumin
Ginger
Juniper
Nutmeg
Sassafras
Star anise
Vanilla bean

ADD FOR COLOUR AND INTEREST

Bergamot (bee balm)
Borage
Coreopsis
Cornflower
Delphinium
Geranium
Gypsophila
Helichrysum (strawflower)
Johnny jump-up
Marigold (calendula)
Nasturtium
Pansy
Statice
Yarrow
Violet

EATING ROSES

Roses are edible; as well as the fruit or hip that forms if the spent blossom is not removed from the plant, the petals, too, can be eaten. Never eat a rose, rose hip, or any edible flower that has been sprayed with any chemicals or been treated with systemic chemicals. Eat only organically grown roses; florist roses are never to be eaten.

Rose hips

Rose hips, as the fruit of roses are called, have been eaten for millennia. When a rose is picked for whatever reason, there cannot be fruit from that rose, as the hip develops from the fertilized flower. The slightly bitter pulp of the rose hip when blended with sugar was, for centuries, a commonly prescribed panacea. Today, rose hips are used in many herbal teas, jams and jellies.

During World War II, it was discovered just how valuable as a fruit wild rose hips are. They have more than 30 times the Vitamin C of orange juice. They are also a good source of vitamins A, B, E and K, and the minerals calcium, phosphorus and iron. The best-tasting rose hips are those of the *Rosa rugosa* and *Rosa canina* and other species shrub roses.

Prepare as you would regular tea, steeping for at least three minutes. For added sweetness, serve with rose sugar.

Edible flowers

Flowers as edibles are gaining in popularity today, yet it was the Romans who first introduced flower eating to Europe, much to the chagrin of the peasants, who used the rose hips.

Rose petals have long been a favourite of herbalists for their purported medicinal qualities. Dried petals of the Apothecary's Rose (*Rosa gallica*) were used for their astringent and tonic qualities. Rose petal conserve was considered a digestive aid. Syrup made from the Damask Rose (*Rosa damascena*) was used as a purgative. Rose vinegar was a common headache remedy. Rose water is used in several Indian desserts and in the confection called Turkish delight.

Only fragrant roses have flavourful petals, but some leave a metallic aftertaste, so sample any rose before using it in the kitchen. As you remove each petal from the flower, notice that the base of the petal is whitish. Remove this part, as it is bitter.

LEFT *Rose hips, like these from* Rosa rugosa, *are edible and an excellent source of vitamin C.*
~

ABOVE *Spread rose petal butter on thinly sliced bread for dainty tea sandwiches.*
~

ABOVE A profusion of rose petals ready for drying, the first stage in assembling a pot-pourri.
~

Rose sugar

Use this sugar in baking for a lovely light rose flavour. Increase the rose flavour by adding rose water to any confection.

1 cup white sugar
2 cups rose petals, shredded (minced)

- Pound sugar and minced rose petals with a pestle and mortar.
- Place in a covered jar for one week.
- Sift, if desired, and store in an airtight container.

ABOVE Carrot slaw served on a bed of rose petals – as delicious as it is attractive.
~

Rose petal butter

Spread on bread for elegant, open sandwiches, or use to baste chicken or fish. Substitute it for plain butter in a favourite cake or biscuit (cookie) recipe.

1 cup fresh rose petals, chopped
¾ cup/200 g/7 oz unsalted (sweet) butter, softened

Mix flowers with butter. Let stand at room temperature for at least 2 hours.

Cover and refrigerate at least 24 hours to let the rose flavour meld into the butter. It may be kept refrigerated up to 2 weeks, or frozen for several months. Freezing may discolour some varieties of roses.

Carrot slaw with rose petals

4 large carrots, grated
1 small courgette (zucchini), grated
½ cup raisins
½ cup mayonnaise
1 tsp celery seed
1 tbsp balsamic vinegar or other herbal vinegar
rose petals

- Mix all ingredients except rose petals together. For the best flavour, refrigerate for several hours before serving.
- Serve on a bed of rose petals (cream-coloured roses look especially elegant). Spoon a small amount of slaw onto a rose petal and enjoy.

A TO Z OF ROSES

Botanically speaking, roses are members of the rose family, Rosaceae. The rose family comprises more than 100 genera of trees, shrubs and herbaceous plants that share similar characteristics. It includes pears, cotoneasters, cherries, pyracantha, raphiolepsis, strawberries, lady's mantle, filipendula, spirea and thousands of other species. All roses are in the genus *Rosa*. There are about 2,000 species of roses and over 20,000 cultivated varieties.

This A to Z is, by necessity, an abbreviated listing of about 120 roses; they are not only some of my personal favourites, but also those of numerous rosarians. If you are looking for a particular characteristic, such as colour, fragrance, disease-resistance and the like, refer to the charts that list recommended roses under these various headings. These charts recommend many roses that could not be fully described in this A to Z section. For inclusion in the garden, first choose those varieties that appear in the A to Z and then extend your selection using roses listed in the charts. If you exhaust even this choice, there are many thousands more varieties available from stockists.

The A to Z is subdivided into eight sections, one for each of the major rose classifications: species roses, old garden roses, modern shrub roses, floribundas and polyanthas, floribundas 'hybrid-tea' type (grandifloras), hybrid teas, climbers and ramblers, and miniatures. The scientific name for the species or the variety name (in quotes) is given first, followed by alternative names. Each entry carries a brief description, a photograph to identify the colour and form of the bloom, and a chart highlighting particular information.

OPPOSITE The names of these climbing roses have been lost to history. This arbour was planted in 1905 and the roses are still thriving today.
~

KEY TO CHART DATA

Indicates the upper-average size of the flower.

Describes the type of bloom: single, semi-double, double or very double (*see* Glossary for definitions).

Details any diseases to which the rose is susceptible.

Indicates varieties which are not winter hardy and require protection.

Denotes award-winning varieties, detailing the award, the awarding body and the year conferred, where applicable.

Indicates the height of the plant. Some varieties achieve a common average height and others fall within a specified range.

ROSE AWARDS AND ROSE SOCIETIES

AARS	All-America Rose Selections
AE, ARS	Award of Excellence, America Rose Society
AGM, RHS	Award of Garden Merit, The Royal Horticultural Society, London
AM, RHS	Award of Merit, The Royal Horticultural Society, London
BBGM	Baden Baden Gold Medal
BGM	Bagatelle Gold Medal, Paris
CM, RNRS	Certificate of Merit, The Royal National Rose Society, St Albans, England (includes National Rose Society awards prior to 1965)
DFP, ARS	David Fuerstenberg Prize, American Rose Society
GGM	Geneva Gold Medal
GM, RNRS	Gold Medal, The Royal National Rose Society, St Albans, England (includes National Rose Society awards prior to 1965)
GMHGA, ARS	Gertrude M Hubbard Gold Award, American Rose Society
GRH	Golden Rose of the Hague
GTAB	Golden Thorn Award, Belfast
HGM	The Hague Gold Medal
JAGRFM, ARS	James Alexander Gamble Rose Fragrance Medal, American Rose Society
NGMC, ARS	National Gold Medal Certificate, American Rose Society
PGM	Portland Gold Medal, USA
PIT, RHS	President's International Trophy, The Royal National Rose Society, St Albans, England (includes National Rose Society awards prior to 1965)
RB	Roeulx, Belgium (prize for the most fragrant rose)
RGM	Rome Gold Medal
ROY, ARS	Rose of the Year, American Rose Society
TGC, AARS	Trial Ground Certificate, The Royal National Rose Society, St Albans, England (includes National Rose Society awards prior to 1965)

SPECIES ROSES

Species roses are those that occur naturally in the wild. They are found throughout the Northern Hemisphere from east to west, but not south of the equator. Species roses hybridize freely in the wild. There are at least 200 wild roses known today. Most species have single flowers with five petals. They self-pollinate, and form hips which produce seeds that will grow true to the parent plant.

On the whole, species roses bloom once, early in the season. This bloom is quite spectacular as the plant produces a large quantity of flowers. The beauty of the species roses does not fade with the flowers. Following the flowers are the brightly coloured hips which are attractive to us and to birds.

Species roses are fairly easy to grow, requiring little care. They are vigorous, but some are more cold tolerant than others. Some species can grow very large, up to 2.7m (9ft) tall by 2.7m (9ft) wide. Others sprawl, making them suitable as ground covers, while some are good hedge material.

Rosa banksiae
LADY BANKS' ROSE

~

First introduced in 1824, this vigorous rose was named after the wife of the director of Kew Gardens near London. There are two forms – 'Lutea' (yellow) and white 'Alba Plena' (also known as *R. banksiae banksiae*). The 2.5–4cm (1–1½in) flowers are double and in large clusters. A mildly fragrant rose, it blooms from late spring to early summer. The canes are very long; this rose can grow to 7.5m (25ft) or more. It is especially striking when trained on large arches or tall pillars. It is resistant to disease and aphids.

Rosa chinensis viridiflora
GREEN ROSE

~

This very unusual rose was introduced before 1845. The petals have become sepals, giving rise to the common name – green rose. It blooms continuously, with 4–6cm (1½–2½in) double flowers. An upright shrub, it grows to 1.2m (4ft) tall. A good container plant, it is disease resistant, but not winter hardy.

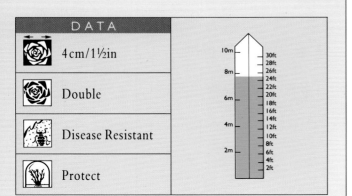

DATA	
4cm/1½in	10m — 30ft, 28ft, 26ft; 8m — 24ft, 22ft, 20ft, 18ft, 16ft; 6m — 14ft, 12ft, 10ft; 4m — 8ft, 6ft; 2m — 4ft, 2ft
Double	
Disease Resistant	
Protect	

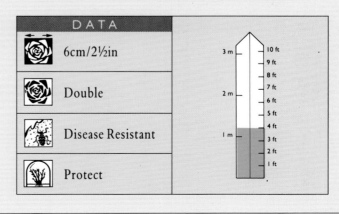

DATA	
6cm/2½in	3 m — 10 ft, 9 ft, 8 ft, 7 ft; 2 m — 6 ft, 5 ft, 4 ft; 1 m — 3 ft, 2 ft, 1 ft
Double	
Disease Resistant	
Protect	

Rosa eglanteria

SWEET BRIAR ROSE, COMMON SWEET BRIAR
~

Also known as Shakespeare's Eglantine, this rose was introduced before 1551. The 2.5–4cm (1–1½in) single flowers are light pink with a true rose smell. Blooming in late spring and early summer, it is not recurrent. The flowers are in clusters, with each flower opening completely, showing attractive yellow stamens. The flowers are followed by oval, bright-red hips. It grows 2.4–3m (8–10ft) tall as an upright shrub with glossy foliage. Relatively disease free, it does get galls, for which it has been prized. In Victorian times, the galls, which have the same fresh apple scent as the foliage, were used in tussy-mussies (fragrant nosegays).

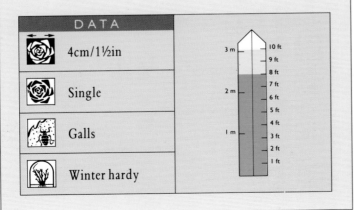

DATA	
4cm/1½in	3 m — 10 ft, 9 ft, 8 ft, 7 ft
Single	2 m — 6 ft, 5 ft, 4 ft
Galls	1 m — 3 ft, 2 ft, 1 ft
Winter hardy	

Rosa multiflora
~

Introduced prior to 1868, this rose is the ancestor of many polyantha and floribunda roses. With 1cm (½in) single, white flowers in large clusters, it blooms early to mid-season. It is not recurrent. The blooms have a honey-like fragrance. Tiny round red hips follow in late summer. Ranging from 2–3.5m to (7–12ft) tall, it can be a successful hedge, but has become a noxious weed in some areas. Most often it is used as an understock, as it is disease free and very winter hardy.

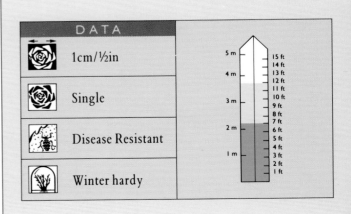

DATA	
1cm/½in	5 m — 15 ft, 14 ft, 13 ft, 12 ft, 11 ft, 10 ft; 4 m — 9 ft, 8 ft
Single	3 m — 7 ft, 6 ft, 5 ft
Disease Resistant	2 m — 4 ft; 1 m — 3 ft, 2 ft, 1 ft
Winter hardy	

Rosa multiflora watsoniana
BAMBOO ROSE

~

This was originally a sport or natural mutant of the floriferous *R. multiflora*. Not a typical rose in appearance, the leaflets are long and narrow, borne on long arching canes. When available, it is grown as a specimen plant or as a botanical curiosity, for its resemblance to bamboo.

Rosa pomifera
APPLE ROSE

~

Introduced in 1771, its common name of apple rose refers to the large hips rather than any fragrance. It blooms early in the season, having 5cm (2in) single, rose-pink flowers with slightly crinkled petals. It grows up to 2.1m (7ft) and has blue-green foliage. Disease free, it is also winter hardy.

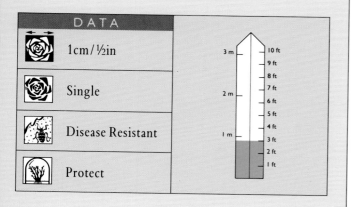

DATA	
1cm / ½in	3 m — 10 ft
Single	2 m — 7 ft
Disease Resistant	1 m — 3 ft
Protect	

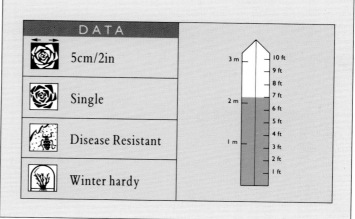

DATA	
5cm/2in	3 m — 10 ft
Single	2 m — 7 ft
Disease Resistant	1 m — 3 ft
Winter hardy	

Rosa rugosa
JAPANESE ROSE, RAMANAS ROSE, RUGOSA ROSE

~

Although native to Asia, this rose has become naturalized in the northeastern United States, especially along the beaches in New England, where it is often referred to as the beach rose. It blooms continuously with very fragrant (with a touch of cinnamon to the scent), carmine, 9–10cm (3½–4in) lightly crinkled flowers that continue even after the large red hips are set. The tart but tasty hips are a good source of vitamin C. A good plant for a hedge, it is spreading, reaching a height of 1.5m (5ft). The deep green leaves are furrowed (rugose). A hardy, disease-resistant plant, it adds an informal accent to a garden. *Rosa rugosa alba,* a sport of *R. rugosa,* only differs in the white colour and strong clove fragrance of the flowers. It was introduced in 1845. *Rosa rugosa rubra,* another sport of *R. rugosa,* was introduced in 1845 and has deeper coloured and more intensely fragrant flowers.

Rosa sericea pteracantha
WINGTHORN ROSE

~

An unusual looking rose, it is grown for its large (up to 2cm (¾in) at the base), translucent, triangular crimson thorns and a multitude of tiny crimson thorns that are prominent along the entire length of year-old branches. On older branches, the thorns turn a dull greyish-brown, so prune back hard after flowering. Cut out old flowering branches to encourage new branches with their attractive thorns. Place this rose where it gets maximum light to highlight the thorns throughout the day and season.

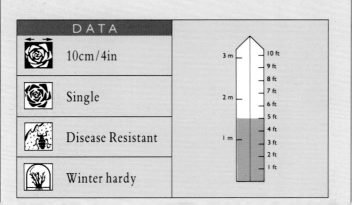

DATA	
10cm/4in	3 m — 10 ft / 9 ft / 8 ft
Single	2 m — 7 ft / 6 ft / 5 ft
Disease Resistant	1 m — 4 ft / 3 ft / 2 ft
Winter hardy	1 ft

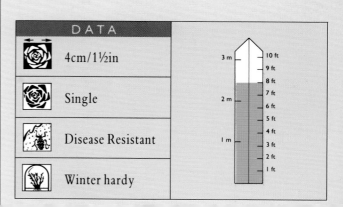

DATA	
4cm/1½in	3 m — 10 ft / 9 ft / 8 ft
Single	2 m — 7 ft / 6 ft / 5 ft
Disease Resistant	1 m — 4 ft / 3 ft / 2 ft
Winter hardy	1 ft

Rosa spinosissima
BURNET ROSE, SCOTCH ROSE
~

Cultivated before 1600, this is a very early blooming non-recurrent rose. A spreading, bushy plant, it only grows to 90cm (3ft) in height. The single or semi-double 4–5cm (1½–2in) flowers vary in colour from white and cream to pale yellow and pink to deep mauve and purple, and have a very mild fragrance. One of the distinguishing features of this rose is the striking small, round, deep purple or black hips that follow the non-recurrent flowers. It grows well in sandy soil, is winter hardy and is disease resistant.

DATA	
5cm/2in	
Single/ semi-double	
Disease Resistant	
Winter hardy	

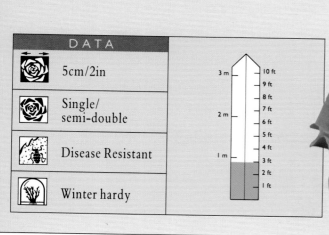

MOST FRAGRANT ROSES

This list is restricted to modern roses. Many old garden roses are very fragrant: gallica roses, for example, keep their fragrance when dried for pot-pourri.

'America' (Cl)
'Angel Face' (F)
'Apricot Nectar' (F)
'Arizona' (Gr)
'Beauty Secret' (Min)
'Blossomtime' (Cl)
'Candy Stripe' (HT)
'Chrysler Imperial' (HT)
'Command Performance' (HT)
'Confidence' (HT)
'Crimson Glory' (HT & Cl)
'Don Juan' (Cl)
'Double Delight' (HT)
'Electron' ('Mullard Jubilee') (HT)
'Fragrant Cloud' (HT)
'Granada' (HT)
'Heirloom' (HT)
'Iceberg' (F)
'Mirandy' (HT)
'Mister Lincoln' (HT)

'Oklahoma' (HT)
'Ole' (Gr)
'Papa Melland' (HT)
'Perfume Delight' (HT)
'Proud Land' (HT)
'Red Fountain' (Cl)
'Rose Parade' (F)
'Royal Highness' (HT)
'Royal Sunset' (Cl)
'Rubaiyat' (HT)
'Saratoga' (F)
'Seashell' (HT)
'Spanish Sun' (F)
'Spartan' (F & Cl)
'Sterling Silver' (HT & Cl)
'Sundowner' (Gr)
'Sunsprite' ('Korresia') (F)
'Tiffany' (HT)
'Tropicana' ('Super Star') (HT)
'White Lightnin'' (Gr)

**KEY: CL — CLIMBER OR RAMBLER   F — FLORIBUNDA
GR — GRANDIFLORA   HT — HYBRID TEA   MIN — MINIATURE**

BELOW 'Mister Lincoln' is popular for its heavy, rich fragrance as well as its velvety red colour.
~

OLD GARDEN ROSES

It is a matter of much debate, what roses should be considered to be old garden roses. Whether the China and tea roses should be in a separate classification from the European varieties and from the varieties that arose from their subsequent hybridization is a matter for the scholars. The subclasses of old garden roses include Gallica, damask, alba, moss, centifolia, Portland, China, tea, Bourbon, Noisette, and hybrid perpetual.

The American Rose Society decreed that time should judge which roses are considered old garden varieties. Any roses in a class that was established before 1867 are thus deemed old garden roses, even if the particular variety was not introduced until after that date. Why 1867? That was the year that La France, one of the first hybrid tea roses, was introduced, thus ushering in the era of the modern roses (hybrid teas, floribundas and grandifloras).

ABOVE *'Salet', introduced in 1854, is a beautiful rosy-pink old garden rose belonging to the subclass of moss roses.*

~

GALLICA ROSES

Gallicas, or French roses, are ancient roses which were cultivated by the Romans. *Rosa gallica* hybridized easily with other roses, and had many natural variations, sporting freely. The colour ranged through the pinks from pale pink to deepest maroon, solid, mottled and striped. From the 1100s to the beginning of the 1800s these were the main roses in cultivation.

They have few thorns, but abundant prickles. The leaves are usually dark green above and softly downy on the reverse. They are upright, fragrant roses and the aroma of the petals intensifies upon drying, so they are an excellent choice for use in pot-pourri (*see* chapter 4). Not recurrent, they have attractive hips in the autumn.

Rosa gallica officinalis
APOTHECARY'S ROSE, RED ROSE OF LANCASTER

~

No date can be set for the introduction of this ancient rose which is believed to be a sport of the species *R. gallica*. Its popularity has continued for centuries, for a variety of reasons. Early herbalists and doctors dried the petals and made them into conserves and syrups. Powdered, the petals were used in a wide range of herbal remedies. The Apothecary's Rose was used much as aspirin is today, as a cure-all. It was the emblem of the House of Lancaster during the English Wars of the Roses in the 1400s. It grows up to 1.2m (4ft) tall, with an upright habit. The flowers are bright crimson with a purple cast, 9–11.5cm (3½–4½in) across, semi-double, opening to show bright gold stamens in the centre. The plant suckers freely, so can be turned into a low thicket in a few years. It is disease resistant and winter hardy.

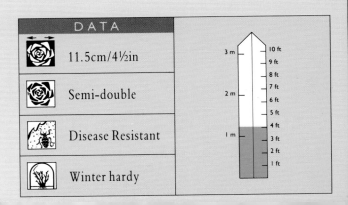

DATA	
11.5cm/4½in	3 m — 10 ft / 9 ft / 8 ft
Semi-double	2 m — 7 ft / 6 ft / 5 ft
Disease Resistant	1 m — 4 ft / 3 ft
Winter hardy	2 ft / 1 ft

'Tuscany Superb'
~

A sport of 'Tuscany', introduced prior to 1848, this rose grows
to 1.2m (4ft) tall. The flowers are crimson-maroon, semi-double,
and 9–10cm (3½–4in) across, with a mild fragrance. It blooms
mid-season, and is not recurrent. It is a compact plant, with a
rounded upright habit. The leaves are rough, and dark green in
colour. It is disease resistant and winter hardy.

DATA	
10cm/4in	
Semi-double	
Disease Resistant	
Winter hardy	

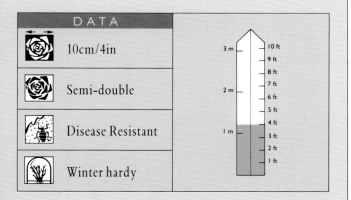

DAMASK ROSES

These hybrids are ancient indeed, grown in Roman hot-houses
to provide blooms all year round. The species *Rosa damascena* is
the main source of attar of roses. The summer damask roses
(hybrids of *R. gallica* and *R. phoenicea*) bloom only once, while
the autumn damasks (hybrids of *R. gallica* and *R. moschata*) have
a second flush of bloom in the autumn. Damask roses are not
very winter hardy, and grow up to 2.1m (7ft) tall, with a range
of white and pink, large fragrant flowers. Leaves are grey-green
and the stems are covered with hooked prickles. Hips are pear-
shaped and bristled.

Rosa damascena semperflorens
ROSE DES QUATRES SAISONS, ROSE OF CASTILE
~

This very fragrant rose is extremely old, and may be the original
autumn damask rose. It grows to 1.2m (4ft), blooming in early
summer and again in early to mid-autumn. The 7.5–9cm (3–
3½in) flowers are richly fragrant, deep pink, and double. It is
winter hardy, but is not recurrent in very cold climates.

DATA	
9cm/3½in	
Double	
Disease Resistant	
Winter hardy	

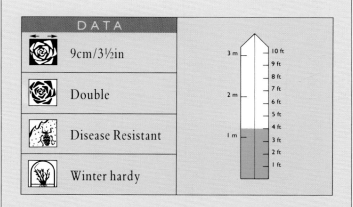

Rosa damascena versicolor (*R. damascena variegata*)
YORK AND LANCASTER ROSE, TUDOR ROSE
~

A very old rose, dating to 1551, it has some white petals and some pink petals, the quantity of each varying from flower to flower. Some flowers may be all white, others are all pink, and some a mixture of both. The mixture of the colours was a symbol of the joining of the Houses of York and Lancaster at the end of the Wars of the Roses. The 6–7.5cm (2½–3in) flowers are double, fragrant and not recurrent. Growing to 1.2m (4ft) tall, it is a bushy rose, which needs attention to keep it thriving. The canes are bristly on this disease-free, winter-hardy rose.

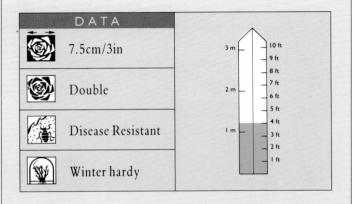

DATA	
7.5cm/3in	
Double	
Disease Resistant	
Winter hardy	

'Pink Leda'
~

Introduced before 1844, this rose tends to trail its 90cm (3ft) canes unless supported. It is attractive on a low trellis or a split-rail fence. The 6–7.5cm (2½–3in) very double flowers are fragrant, blooming mid-season, but are not recurrent. The canes are thorny and foliage is a handsome dark greyish-green. It is winter hardy and disease free. 'Leda', similar in habit, but with white flowers lightly edged in red, is also known as the 'Painted Damask'.

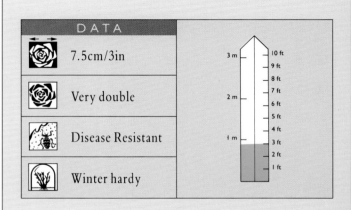

DATA	
7.5cm/3in	
Very double	
Disease Resistant	
Winter hardy	

ALBA ROSES

Alba roses are believed to be descended from *Rosa canina* and *R. damascena*. The flowers are usually small, white to pale pink, very fragrant, single or double, borne in small clusters, and non-recurrent. They were described in literature by Pliny, and were believed to have been cultivated by the Romans. Albas are tall, upright plants with soft, downy, greyish foliage and thorny canes.

'Felicité Parmentier'

~

This shrub, which grows to 1.2m (4ft), was introduced in 1836. Blooming in early summer, it flowers freely, but is not recurrent. The double flowers are about 6cm (2½in), and white to pale salmon in the centre. As it opens the petals reflex, so the impression is of a globose white flower. The foliage is less grey than other alba roses.

Rosa x alba

WHITE ROSE OF YORK

~

One of the oldest garden roses, it has semi-double white or pale pink flowers in early summer that are not recurrent. A vigorous and prickly shrub, it can grow to 2.4m (8ft).

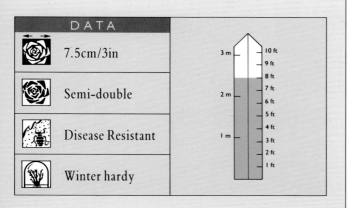

DATA		
7.5cm/3in		3 m — 10 ft / 9 ft / 8 ft
Semi-double		2 m — 7 ft / 6 ft / 5 ft
Disease Resistant		1 m — 4 ft / 3 ft
Winter hardy		2 ft / 1 ft

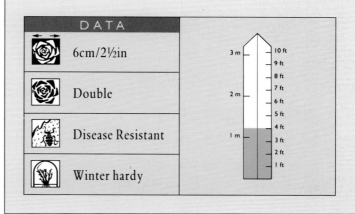

DATA		
6cm/2½in		3 m — 10 ft / 9 ft / 8 ft
Double		2 m — 7 ft / 6 ft / 5 ft
Disease Resistant		1 m — 4 ft / 3 ft
Winter hardy		2 ft / 1 ft

MOSS ROSES

Moss roses get their name from the small hair-like glands on the sepals that resemble moss. The gland is sticky, giving off a pleasant pine scent when touched. Moss roses have two ancestors. Those that are sports of centifolias have green moss on the stem and calyx, while the sports of the damask perpetuals have thinner brownish moss and are recurrent bloomers. Moss rose-buds were popular in Victorian times, often included in a tussy-mussy (a fragrant nosegay) for their unique appearance and aroma. The flowers are double, with inward-curving petals, and are most often shades of pink, but some hybrids are much deeper coloured crimson or purple. The canes, which turn from red to green as they age, have long straight thorns. Most grow to less than 1.5m (5ft), but some can grow to 3m (10ft) with support.

Rosa centifolia muscosa
COMMON MOSS, COMMUNIS, OLD PINK MOSS

~

A sport of *R. centifolia*, this old rose was introduced in 1696. The clear pink flowers are well scented, double, and very full with tightly packed petals, 5–7.5cm (2–3in) across. This rose is not recurrent. The sepals are fringed, with heavy moss on the calyx and stem. A hardy, vigorous plant, it can grow to 1.8m (6ft) tall. Dark green, sparse leaves are borne on heavily bristled canes. This rose has withstood the test of time, and is still the most popular of the moss roses.

'William Lobb'
'DUCHESSE D'ISTRIE', OLD VELVET MOSS

~

Introduced in 1855, the buds of this centifolia rose are very mossy with a strong pine aroma. The semi-double flowers, 5–7.5cm (2–3in) across, are crimson, but fade to greyish-mauve as they age. The fragrant blooms are mid-season, and not recurrent. A tall, thorny bush, it can grow upwards of 2.4m (8ft) tall, and is best supported on a pillar.

DATA	
7.5cm/3in	
Double	
Mildew	
Winter hardy	

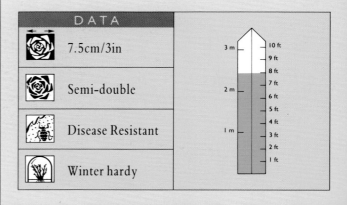

DATA	
7.5cm/3in	
Semi-double	
Disease Resistant	
Winter hardy	

CENTIFOLIA ROSES

Centifolia roses are also known as cabbage roses as the bloom resembles a head of cabbage with large petals opened around tightly packed smaller petals. *Rosa × centifolia* is found in Provence, France, giving rise to the other common name, Provence Rose. Very fragrant, these hybrids were a popular flower in the late 1700s and early 1800s. The canes are long and heavily thorned, with sparse foliage. Cabbage roses are grown in France commercially as a source of attar of roses, the essential oil that is distilled from fresh rose petals.

Rosa centifolia cristata
CRESTED MOSS ROSE

~

Not a true moss rose, but with a mossy-looking fringe on the margins of the sepals, it was introduced in 1827. Still popular for its unique buds as well as its very double medium-pink flowers, it blooms fragrantly in mid-season but is not recurrent. It grows upright from 1·5–2·1m (5–7ft) tall with an open habit. It is disease resistant and winter hardy.

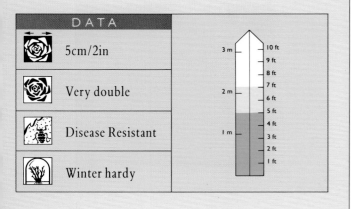

DATA		
🌹	5cm/2in	
🌹	Very double	
🐞	Disease Resistant	
🌿	Winter hardy	

'Vierge de Cléry'

~

Introduced in 1888, this cabbage rose has red buds that open into double, fragrant, 5–7.5cm (2–3in), white flowers, often with a tinge of red at the edge of some outer petals. Growing to 1.5m (5ft), it blooms in late summer, after most of the other cabbage roses are past. It is very winter hardy.

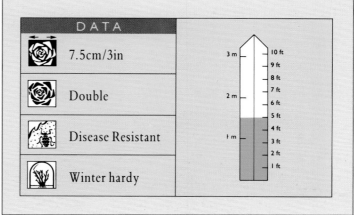

DATA		
🌹	7.5cm/3in	
🌹	Double	
🐞	Disease Resistant	
🌿	Winter hardy	

CHINA AND TEA ROSES

Until the introduction of the China and tea roses in the late 1700s, Europeans were not familiar with recurrent roses; their varieties bloomed only once. Both the China (*Rosa chinensis*) and the tea (*R. odorata*) were recurrent bloomers. The tea rose, which also comes from China, gets its name from the fragrance of the flowers which is reminiscent of crushed tea leaves. Neither species or hybrids are seen much in cultivation, but their characteristic recurrent flowering was bred into the hybrid perpetuals and polyanthas, and carried into the modern hybrid tea rose. China roses are small bushes with few thorns. Not hardy, they are successfully wintered over indoors. Tea roses can be dwarf shrubs or vigorous climbers.

ABOVE '*Papillon*', *a China rose.*
~

'*Catherine Mermet*'
~

Introduced in 1869, this tea rose has 5–7.5cm (2–3in) double blossoms of pale flesh pink, with a lilac hue to the inner petals. The stems tend to be weak, as do those of many teas. A sturdy upright plant with open habit, it grows 90–120cm (3–4ft) tall. The bloom is continuous throughout the growing season. Not winter hardy, even with protection, this rose is disease resistant.

DATA	
7.5cm/3in	
Double	
Disease Resistant	
Tender even with protection	

3 m — 10 ft / 9 ft / 8 ft
2 m — 7 ft / 6 ft / 5 ft
1 m — 4 ft / 3 ft / 2 ft / 1 ft

PORTLAND ROSES

Portland roses, or damask perpetuals, were named in honour of Margaret Cavendish Bentinck, the second Duchess of Portland. 'Duchess of Portland' was the product of a chance cross between a China rose and a damask rose. Damask perpetuals were developed in the early 1800s for their recurrent properties. A number of cultivars were produced, but with the availability of the China and tea roses, further development of these roses stopped, as the China and tea roses were much more reliable as repeat bloomers.

There are not many damask perpetuals today, but those that have endured are good recurrent bloomers, with fully double blooms on short stems. Very fragrant, they are rounded bushes with rich red flowers that bloom late in summer.

BELOW '*Yolande d'Aragon*', *a Portland rose introduced in 1843.*
~

BOURBON ROSES

The Bourbon rose (*R. × borboniana*) was a natural hybrid of the damask and China roses growing on Reunion Island (formerly the Isle of Bourbon) in the Caribbean. Seeds arrived in France in 1819, and cultivation began in earnest. This fragrant pink rose blooms in early and late summer and in autumn (fall). Hybrid Bourbon roses are crosses between *R. odorata*, the tea rose, and this hybrid rose. They are the ancestors of the hybrid perpetual roses which gave rise to the hybrid tea roses.

'Souvenir de la Malmaison'

~

Introduced in 1843, this rose is seen as a compact 60cm (2ft) shrub or a climber to 3m (10ft). A sparse bloomer, with even sparser repeat in the autumn, its pale pink to white, 4–10cm (1½–4in), very double flowers have a spicy fragrance.

DATA	
4–10cm/1½–4in	
Very double	
Disease Resistant	
Winter hardy	

3 m — 10 ft / 9 ft / 8 ft / 7 ft / 6 ft / 5 ft / 4 ft / 3 ft / 2 ft / 1 ft (2 m, 1 m markers)

'Commandant Beaurepaire'

~

A very showy rose, introduced in 1874, it has multi-coloured (white, light pink, crimson) flecks and streaks on deep pink petals. The fragrant double flowers are 7.5–9cm (3–3½in) wide, appearing in mid-season with no repeat bloom to speak of. It grows from 1.2–1.5m (4–5ft) tall in an upright form with few thorns. It is a vigorous, hardy, disease-resistant rose.

NOISETTE ROSES

Noisette or Champney roses (*Rosa × noisettiana*) were the result of a cross between *R. chinensis* and *R. moschata* made in Charleston, South Carolina, by John Champney in the early 1800s. The first cultivar, 'Champney's Pink Cluster' was given to his friend, Philip Noisette, who in turn sent it on to his brother in France. These roses grow well in warm climates, and are not winter hardy. Cultivars range in growth and habit from dwarf roses to vigorous climbers. The flowers are borne in large clusters with up to 100 flowers in a corymb.

DATA	
9cm/3½in	
Double	
Disease Resistant	
Winter hardy	

3 m — 10 ft / 9 ft / 8 ft / 7 ft / 6 ft / 5 ft / 4 ft / 3 ft / 2 ft / 1 ft (2 m, 1 m markers)

HYBRID PERPETUAL ROSES

Hybrid perpetual roses, also called remontant roses, were very popular from 1840 to 1880, with more than 4,000 varieties developed during that time. However, there have been no new hybrid perpetuals introduced in more than 60 years. The name is somewhat misleading, as they are not everblooming, but certainly more recurrent than any other rose of their time. Their ancestry is mixed, with a strong Bourbon, Portland and tea lineage. Hybrid perpetuals are disease resistant and extremely winter hardy. The flowers are large (up to 18cm, or 7in), in colours of crimson, pink and white, and are double and very fragrant. Modern hybrid tea roses are descended from hybrid perpetuals.

'Henry Nevard'
~

Introduced in 1924, this rose is characteristic of the development of the hybrid perpetual towards the modern hybrid tea. The 10–11.5cm (4–4½in) fragrant, deep-crimson, double flowers bloom mid-season, repeating in autumn. The bush grows to 1.5m (5ft), with an upright bushy habit; the leaves are a glossy, deep green. It is disease resistant and winter hardy.

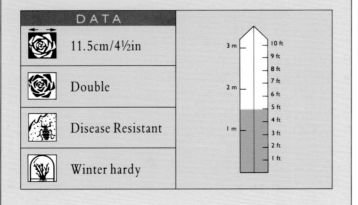

DATA	
11.5cm/4½in	
Double	
Disease Resistant	
Winter hardy	

'Roger Lambelin'
~

This striking rose was introduced in 1890. The flowers are only 6–7cm (2½–3in) wide, but the eye is immediately drawn to this plant. The double maroon flowers, edged in white which occasionally extends into the flower, have a good scent. It blooms mid-season and repeats well in the autumn if the plant is well cultivated. An upright plant with somewhat thorny canes and dark green leaves, it is prone to blackspot. It is winter hardy.

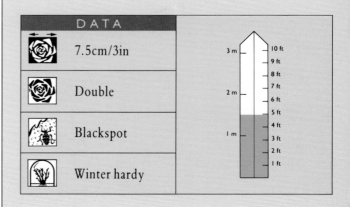

DATA	
7.5cm/3in	
Double	
Blackspot	
Winter hardy	

RED
Rosa gallica officinalis (G)
'Crimson Globe' (M)
'Nuits de Young' (M)
'Souv. d'Alphonse Lavallée'
(HP)

YELLOW
R. banksiae lutea (Sp)
R. hugonis (Sp)

WHITE
'Coquette des Alpes' (B)
'Dupontii' (Misc OGR)
'Leda' (D)
'Mabel Morrison' (HP)
'Mme Hardy' (D)
'Nastarana' (N)
R. banksiae banksiae (Sp)

PINK
'Celsiana' (D)
R. centifolia cristata (C)
'Marie Louise' (D)
'Paul's Early Blush' (HP)
'Rose de Meaux' (Ch)
'Souv. de la Malmaison' (B)

MAUVE
'Celina' (M)
'Charles de Mills' (G)
R. rugosa rubra (Sp)
'Tuscany' (G)

BLEND
'Commandant
Beaurepaire' (B)
'Louis Philippe' (Ch)
'Mutabilis' (Ch)
R. foetida bicolor (Sp)
'William Lobb' (M)

KEY: B — BOURBON   C — CENTIFOLIA   CH — CHINA
D — DAMASK   G — GALLICA   HP — HYBRID PERPETUAL
M — MOSS   MISC OGR — MISCELLANEOUS OLD GARDEN ROSE
N — NOISETTE   SP — SPECIES

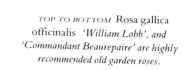

*TOP TO BOTTOM Rosa gallica
officinalis 'William Lobb', and
'Commandant Beaurepaire' are highly
recommended old garden roses.*
~

MODERN SHRUB ROSES

The term 'shrub rose' is perhaps a misnomer, as it does not denote the size, shape, or habit of a rose in this context, but rather a group for classification purposes. The hybrid roses that are in a class that was in existence before 1867 are considered old garden roses; those classified later are modern roses. There are several subclasses of shrub roses: hybrid eglantines, hybrid musks, hybrid rugosas, hybrid spinosissimas (some are old garden roses), and shrub roses. The last class is a catch-all for those roses that do not fall into any of the other four subclasses.

The characteristic that is common to all the shrub roses is their toughness. Some are species that grow true from seed, while others are man-made cultivated varieties. They vary in height from 60cm (2ft) to 3m (10ft). Flowers range through white, pink, red, orange, yellow and purple. The older varieties are not recurrent, but some newer introductions bloom continuously throughout the growing season.

'Alchymist'
~

Introduced in 1956, this shrub rose is attractive when supported on a pillar or trellis. The very double, 9–10cm (3½–4in), fragrant flowers may be quartered. This rose blooms early to mid-season and is not recurrent. The colour is an apricot blend. A vigorous rose, its young leaves are bronze, turning to a glossy dark green as they mature. It is disease resistant and winter hardy.

'Bonica'
'MEIDOMONAC'
~

A modern shrub rose introduced in 1982, this is a handsome, low-growing plant. The 5–7.5cm (2–3in) rose-pink flowers are double. It blooms almost continuously, producing an abundance of bright orange hips late in the season. Its habit is spreading and arching, growing not more than 1m (3½ft) tall. It is disease resistant and winter hardy.

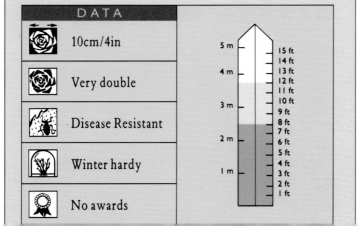

DATA	
🌹	10cm/4in
🌹	Very double
🐞	Disease Resistant
🌱	Winter hardy
🏵	No awards

5 m — 15 ft, 14 ft, 13 ft; 4 m — 12 ft, 11 ft; 3 m — 10 ft, 9 ft, 8 ft; 2 m — 7 ft, 6 ft, 5 ft, 4 ft; 1 m — 3 ft, 2 ft, 1 ft

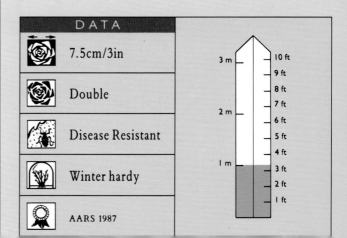

DATA	
🌹	7.5cm/3in
🌹	Double
🐞	Disease Resistant
🌱	Winter hardy
🏵	AARS 1987

3 m — 10 ft, 9 ft, 8 ft, 7 ft; 2 m — 6 ft, 5 ft, 4 ft; 1 m — 3 ft, 2 ft, 1 ft

'Buff Beauty'
~

A hybrid musk rose introduced in 1939, it is vigorous and spreading, growing to 1.8m (6ft) in all directions. The 7.5cm (3in) double flowers, apricot blended with yellow and gold that pale at the edge as they mature, have a delightful fragrance. It blooms mid to late-season and is recurrent through the summer. The foliage is tinged bronze when young, maturing to a glossy medium green. It is disease resistant and winter hardy.

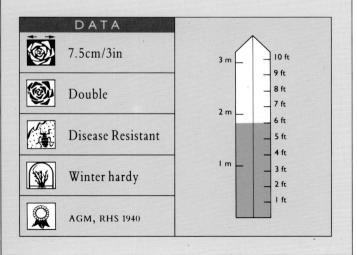

DATA	
🌹	7.5cm/3in
🌹	Double
🐞	Disease Resistant
🌱	Winter hardy
🏵	AGM, RHS 1940

3 m — 10 ft, 9 ft, 8 ft, 7 ft; 2 m — 6 ft, 5 ft, 4 ft; 1 m — 3 ft, 2 ft, 1 ft

'Cécile Brunner'
'MIGNON', 'SWEETHEART ROSE'
~

A polyantha, introduced in 1881, this rose is noted for its small perfect blooms. The lightly fragrant, pale-pink flowers, slightly deeper pink in the centre, and not over 3cm (1¼in) in size, are double, looking like miniature tea roses. It blooms in early summer and is recurrent throughout the rest of the summer. It grows to 1.2m (4ft) with an upright, bushy habit. The abundant leaves are small and dark green with a neat appearance on relatively smooth canes with few thorns. It is disease resistant but not reliably winter hardy. Never prune too hard, only remove weak or dead growth. A perfect rose for a buttonhole.

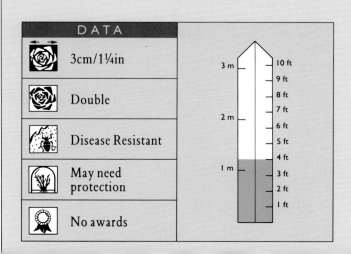

DATA	
🌹	3cm/1¼in
🌹	Double
🐞	Disease Resistant
🌱	May need protection
🏵	No awards

3 m — 10 ft, 9 ft, 8 ft, 7 ft; 2 m — 6 ft, 5 ft, 4 ft; 1 m — 3 ft, 2 ft, 1 ft

'Goldbusch'
~

This modern shrub rose was introduced in 1954. The fragrant double flowers have an open, cupped form, 6–7.5cm (2½–3in) across. The petals are yellow, becoming paler towards the edges. Blooming in mid to late-season, it is recurrent. Its habit is upright and spreading, perfect for training on a pillar. The young leaves are yellowish-green, turning light green as they mature. It is disease resistant and winter hardy.

'Golden Wings'
~

A vigorous modern shrub rose, introduced in 1956, it grows to 1.8m (6ft) in height and width. An early bloomer, it flowers continuously through to autumn. The single, 10–13cm (4–5in) flowers have a slight fragrance, and open fully to reveal gold stamens and red-based filaments. The hips are attractive – orange-red in the autumn. It has a loose habit, is disease resistant and moderately winter hardy.

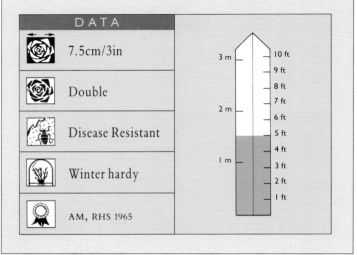

DATA	
🌹	7.5cm/3in
🌹	Double
🐛	Disease Resistant
🌱	Winter hardy
🏅	AM, RHS 1965

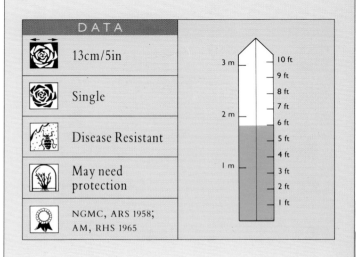

DATA	
🌹	13cm/5in
🌹	Single
🐛	Disease Resistant
🌱	May need protection
🏅	NGMC, ARS 1958; AM, RHS 1965

'Mrs Anthony Waterer'
~

A hybrid rugosa that was introduced in 1898, this rose is covered with fragrant, magenta-crimson flowers in early summer. The 9cm (3½in) semi-double flowers open to reveal the golden stamens at the centre. It is only slightly recurrent in the autumn. The shrub is bushy and spreading, growing to 1.5m (5ft) all around. The leaves are medium green and deeply etched, giving the wrinkled look that is characteristic of rugosas. It is disease resistant and winter hardy. Because of its vibrant colour, it can be difficult to place in the garden, so it is often grown by itself.

'Pink Grootendorst'
~

Introduced in 1923, this hybrid rugosa rose was originally a sport of the red 'F J Grootendorst'. The 4cm (1½in) double flowers are a bright pink that tends to fade in the sun. The petals are slightly fringed. This rose blooms in clusters mid-season, and is recurrent. It grows up to 1.8m (6ft) with an upright vigorous habit. It is disease resistant and winter hardy.

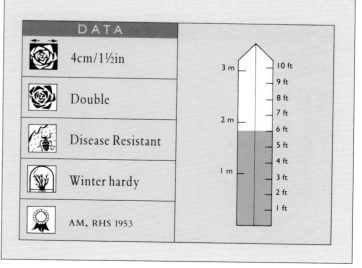

DATA	
4cm/1½in	
Double	
Disease Resistant	
Winter hardy	
AM, RHS 1953	

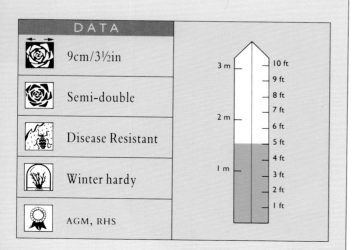

DATA	
9cm/3½in	
Semi-double	
Disease Resistant	
Winter hardy	
AGM, RHS	

'The Fairy'

~

Introduced in 1932, this light-pink polyantha is widely variant. It is seen as a low trailing plant that is an effective groundcover, and as a more upright plant, suitable for hedging or use in the rose garden. The double, cupped flowers are borne on large trusses. It blooms later in the season than many other polyanthas, and repeats well. The leaves are very small, deep green and glossy. It is disease resistant and winter hardy.

DATA	
4cm/1½in	
Double	
Disease Resistant	
Winter hardy	
No awards	

3 m — 10 ft / 9 ft / 8 ft / 7 ft
2 m — 6 ft / 5 ft / 4 ft
1 m — 3 ft / 2 ft / 1 ft

HIGHLY RECOMMENDED SHRUB ROSES

RED
'Dortmund' (K)
'F J Grootendorst' (HRg)
'Hansa' (HRg)
'Summer Wind' (S)
'Will Scarlet' (HMsk)

YELLOW
'Fruhlingsgold' (HSpn)
'Golden Wings' (S)

WHITE
'Blanc Double de Coubert' (HRg)
'Nevada' (HMoy)
'Weisse au Sparrieshoop' (S)

PINK
'Canterbury' (S)
'Cécile Brunner' (Pol)
'Cerise Bouquet' (S)
'China Doll' (Pol)
'Flamingo' (HRg)
'Raubritter' (HMac)
'The Fairy' (Pol)
'Wanderin' Wind' (S)

BLEND
'Alchymist' (S)
'Applejack' (S)
'Cornelia' (HMsk)
'Dr Eckener' (HRg)
'Dornroschen' (S)
'Paulii Rosea' (S)

KEY: HMAC – HYBRID MACRANTHA HMOY – HYBRID MOYESII HMSK – HYBRID MUSK HRG – HYBRID RUGOSA HSPN – HYBRID SPINOSISSIMA K – KORDESII POL – POLYANTHA S – SHRUB

LEFT TO RIGHT 'Cécile Brunner' and 'Golden Wings' are highly recommended shrub roses.
~

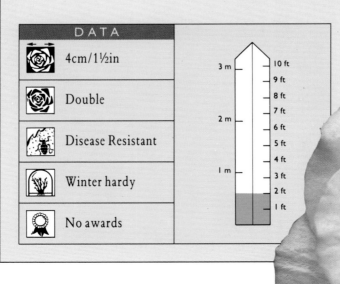

HYBRID TEA ROSES

Hybrid teas are the largest group of modern roses and are still the most widely grown of all roses. Think of a rose and the image that comes to mind usually has the characteristics of the hybrid teas: long pointed buds opening to elegant, high-centred, fragrant flowers of diverse colours on long straight stems.

Hybrid teas are the oldest of the so-called modern roses. In the mid-1800s hybrid perpetuals were the most favoured roses. In general, rose breeders and hybridizers of that time were concerned with creating new hybrid perpetuals. In 1867, J B Guillot was crossing hybrid perpetuals with tea roses. One notably successful result was 'La France'. It had inherited traits from both of its parents, most importantly the recurrent bloom of the tea rose and the hardiness of the hybrid perpetual. At the time it was considered another hybrid perpetual. It was not until 13 years later that it was recognized as the first in a new class of roses, named 'hybrid tea' in recognition of the parentage.

In the late 1880s, Pernet-Ducher in Lyon, France, was successful in introducing the yellow from *Rosa foetida persiana* into hybrid perpetuals. Yellows, golds and oranges were added to the range of colours. The early yellow roses were classed as Pernetianas until the 1930s when they became assimilated by the hybrid teas. Unfortunately, with the brilliant new colours came susceptibility to blackspot.

The firm Brownell of Rhode Island introduced *R. wichuraiana* into the hybrid tea gene pool, with the goal of developing hardier roses that were resistant to blackspot, and succeeded in creating the so-called 'sub-zero' hybrid teas. These in turn were used by Wilhelm Kordes in Germany to raise roses hardy for northern Europe. Today's hybrid teas vary in their hardiness; there are varieties for almost every climate.

Hybrid teas grow from 60–180cm (2–6ft) tall. With their long stems, most are good cut flowers. The buds are long and pointed. Flowers range from single to very double. Most of those introduced in the last 50 years are high-centred. Blooms are usually borne singly; rarely in a cluster of less than six flowers. The foliage is usually thin and dark green. Most hybrid teas are fragrant, with varying scents from that of the true rose to that of tea. Roses are generally most fragrant in the early morning before the volatile oils evaporate with the heat of the day.

Today hybrid teas are the most popular roses, cornering more than 60 per-cent of the world's rose market. Most florist roses are hybrid teas. They are elegant plants, perfect in a formal setting, yet comfortable in a quaint cottage garden. Their beauty, fragrance and form is unsurpassed in any other group of roses.

'American Heritage'

~

Introduced in 1965, the colour of this rose is variable and depends on the climate in which it is grown. The 10–15cm (4–6in) double flowers are a yellow blend with cream and salmon-red. It has a light fragrance. Growing from 1.8–2.4m (6–8ft), it is a vigorous shrub with an upright habit. The large leaves are dark green. It grows best in areas where the summers are hot and dry, as it is susceptible to mildew. It is marginally hardy, needing winter protection.

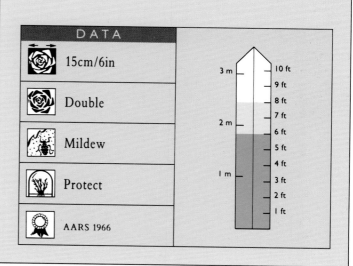

DATA	
15cm/6in	
Double	
Mildew	
Protect	
AARS 1966	

'Brandy'
~

Introduced in 1982, this has a lovely fruity fragrance. The 10–11.5cm (4–4½in) double flowers are an apricot blend. It does not have the typical form of a hybrid tea; it opens fully to reveal bright-yellow stamens. A vigorous shrub, it grows to 1.5m (5ft) with an upright habit. The large leaves are bright green and glossy. It is susceptible to blackspot, but otherwise disease resistant. Marginally hardy, it needs winter protection.

'Broadway'
~

Introduced in 1986, this is a show-stopping rose. The 10–13cm (4–5in) double flowers are a yellow blend with reddish-pink and cream. The flowers are high-centred and fragrant. It blooms well throughout the season. A vigorous plant, it grows from 1.5–1.8m (5–6ft), with an upright habit. It needs winter protection in areas with cold winters.

DATA	
11.5cm/4½in	
Double	
Blackspot	
Protect	
AARS 1982	

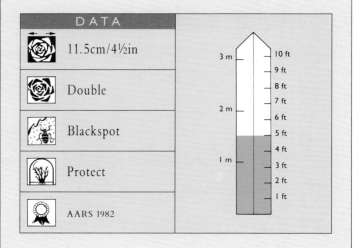

DATA	
13cm/5in	
Double	
Disease Resistant	
Protect in cold areas	
AARS 1986	

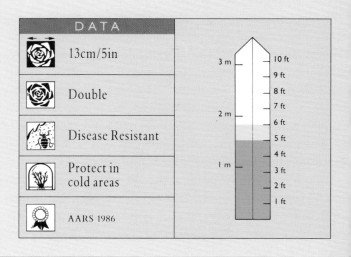

'Charlotte Armstrong'
~

Introduced in 1940, this rose is the ancestor of many of today's award-winning roses, including 'Chrysler Imperial', 'Tiffany', 'Mirandy', 'Garden Party' and 'Sutter's Gold'. The 9–11.5cm (3½–4½in), double flowers open from slender, attractive, blood-red buds. The flower is deep pink with a light fragrance. It blooms early in summer, and is recurrent. A vigorous shrub growing from 1.2–1.5m (4–5ft), it has an upright, compact habit. The large leaves are dark green and leathery. This rose is disease resistant, but needs winter protection in cold areas.

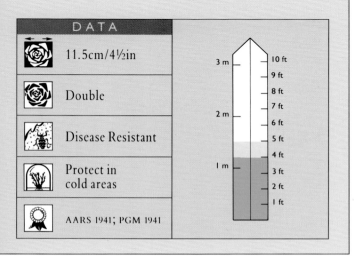

DATA	
11.5cm/4½in	
Double	
Disease Resistant	
Protect in cold areas	
AARS 1941; PGM 1941	

'Chicago Peace'
~

Introduced in 1962, this is a sport of 'Peace'. The 13–14cm (5–5½in) double flowers are a pink blend with apricot and a dominant yellow at the base. The full blooms are mildly fragrant. A vigorous shrub growing 1.3–1.6m (4½–5½ft), it has an upright, well-branched habit. The large leaves are dark green, leathery and glossy. It is disease resistant and winter hardy.

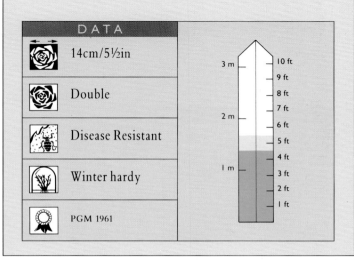

DATA	
14cm/5½in	
Double	
Disease Resistant	
Winter hardy	
PGM 1961	

'Christian Dior'
~

Introduced in 1958, the 10–11.5cm (4–4½in) double flowers are medium red and velvety in appearance, a shade lighter on the reverse. The flowers are high-centred, opening to a very full, cupped form. Blooming abundantly mid-season, it repeats fairly well, and is mildly fragrant. The edges of the petal discolour in the heat of the summer sun, so it is best planted where it gets full morning sun and is somewhat shaded in the afternoon. A vigorous shrub growing 1.2–1.5 (4–5ft) tall, it has an upright, well-branched habit. The large, dark-green leaves are semi-glossy and leathery. It is susceptible to mildew and is tender, needing protection in the winter.

'Chrysler Imperial'
~

Introduced in 1952, this rose is known for its rich spicy fragrance. The 11.5–13cm (4½–5in) double flowers are deep red. They have a classic high-centred form, opening to very full flowers. This rose blooms profusely mid-season and repeats well. It is a good warm climate rose; the colour is not as rich in cool areas. A vigorous shrub to 1.5m (5ft), it has a compact, upright habit. The dark-green leaves are semi-glossy. It is susceptible to mildew and rust. It is winter hardy.

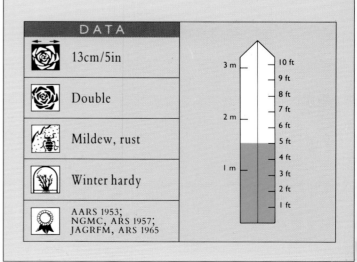

DATA	
13cm/5in	3 m — 10 ft / 9 ft / 8 ft / 7 ft
Double	2 m — 6 ft
Mildew, rust	5 ft / 4 ft
Winter hardy	1 m — 3 ft / 2 ft / 1 ft
AARS 1953; NGMC, ARS 1957; JAGRFM, ARS 1965	

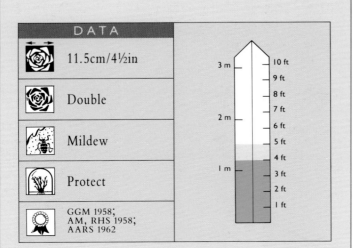

DATA	
11.5cm/4½in	3 m — 10 ft / 9 ft / 8 ft / 7 ft
Double	2 m — 6 ft
Mildew	5 ft / 4 ft
Protect	1 m — 3 ft / 2 ft / 1 ft
GGM 1958; AM, RHS 1958; AARS 1962	

'Colour Magic'
~

Introduced in 1978, this rose changes colour each day. The buds are ivory pink, opening to high-centred, deep pink, sweetly-scented 13–15cm (5–6in) blooms. As the flowers mature, they become cupped, with the ivory and red developing prominence. This rose blooms well throughout the season. A vigorous shrub to 1.2m (4ft), it has an upright and well-branched habit. The large leaves are dark green and semi-glossy. It is disease resistant and needs winter protection in cold areas.

'Command Performance'
~

Introduced in 1970, this rose fairly glows in the garden. The double 13–15cm (5–6in) flowers are a muted orange. They have a classic, high-centred form and a strong fragrance. Blooming prolifically throughout the season, the flowers are borne singly or in clusters. A vigorous shrub to 1.5m (5ft), it has an upright habit. The leaves are green and leathery. It is susceptible to mildew, and the flowers may become distorted in hot humid weather. It is winter hardy with protection.

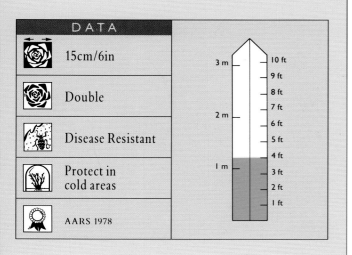

DATA	
15cm/6in	3 m — 10 ft / 9 ft / 8 ft / 7 ft
Double	2 m — 6 ft / 5 ft
Disease Resistant	4 ft
Protect in cold areas	1 m — 3 ft / 2 ft / 1 ft
AARS 1978	

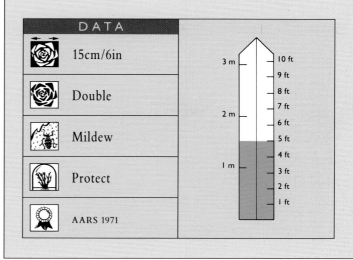

DATA	
15cm/6in	3 m — 10 ft / 9 ft / 8 ft / 7 ft
Double	2 m — 6 ft / 5 ft
Mildew	4 ft
Protect	1 m — 3 ft / 2 ft / 1 ft
AARS 1971	

'Dainty Bess'
~

Introduced in 1925, this hybrid tea is enjoying a resurgence of popularity. The 9cm (3½in) single flowers are light to medium rose-pink, opening flat to reveal handsome maroon stamens. Free-flowering continuously throughout the season, the freshly fragrant blossoms are borne singly or in clusters. Growing to 1m (3½ft), it has an upright, well-branched habit. The medium-green leaves are leathery and semi-glossy. It is disease resistant and winter hardy. There is a climbing form.

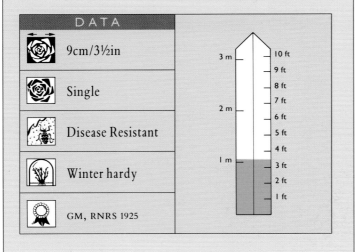

DATA	
9cm/3½in	
Single	
Disease Resistant	
Winter hardy	
GM, RNRS 1925	

3 m / 10 ft / 9 ft / 8 ft / 7 ft / 2 m / 6 ft / 5 ft / 4 ft / 1 m / 3 ft / 2 ft / 1 ft

'Dolly Parton'
~

Introduced in 1983, this rose is as colourful as its namesake. The 11.5–13cm (4½–5in) double flowers are orange-red. They have a high-centred form, and are very fragrant. This rose blooms continuously throughout the season. A vigorous shrub to 1.3m (4½ft), it has an upright, well-branched habit. New leaves are dark red, turning glossy, dark green as they mature. It is disease resistant and winter hardy with protection.

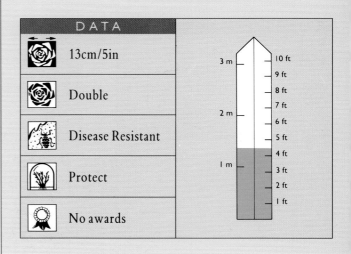

DATA	
13cm/5in	
Double	
Disease Resistant	
Protect	
No awards	

3 m / 10 ft / 9 ft / 8 ft / 7 ft / 2 m / 6 ft / 5 ft / 4 ft / 1 m / 3 ft / 2 ft / 1 ft

'Double Delight'

~

Introduced in 1977, this rose is a delight for its changing colour and its intense, spicy fragrance. The 14cm (5½in) double flowers are bicoloured. They open creamy-white with red edging, gradually becoming redder as they mature. The flowers have a classic high-centred form, and are long-lasting when cut. This rose blooms profusely throughout the season. A vigorous shrub to 1.2m (4ft), it has a spreading, very bushy, upright habit. The medium-green leaves are semi-glossy. This rose is susceptible to mildew in cool damp climates, but is otherwise disease resistant and winter hardy.

'Eclipse'

~

Introduced in 1935, the name of this rose commemorates the solar eclipse of 31 August 1932. The 9–10cm (3½–4in) double flowers are medium yellow, with an open, loose form. It blooms profusely mid-season and is recurrent. It has a mild fragrance. A vigorous shrub to 1.2m (4ft), it has an upright, bushy form. The dark-green leaves are thick and leathery. It is disease resistant, but needs winter protection.

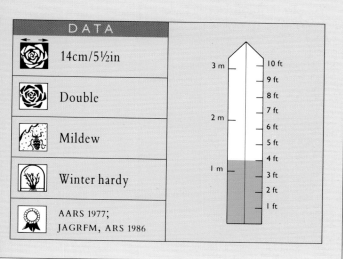

DATA	
14cm/5½in	
Double	
Mildew	
Winter hardy	
AARS 1977; JAGRFM, ARS 1986	

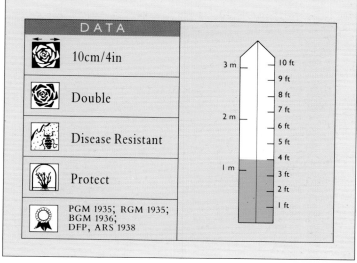

DATA	
10cm/4in	
Double	
Disease Resistant	
Protect	
PGM 1935; RGM 1935; BGM 1936; DFP, ARS 1938	

'Electron'
'MULLARD JUBILEE'
~

Introduced in 1970, the blooms of this rose are almost electric pink. The 13cm (5in) double flowers are strongly fragrant, with a classic high-centred form. This rose begins to bloom later than most hybrid teas, but blooms abundantly and continuously, even in the heat of the summer. A vigorous shrub to 1m (3½ft), it has a full, bushy habit. The medium-green, leathery leaves are closely spaced, covering the plant to ground level.

'First Prize'
~

Introduced in 1970, this is one of the top ten roses rated by the American Rose Society. The 13–15cm (5–6in) double flowers are a pink blend with ivory. They have a high-centred form, are moderately fragrant with an old-fashioned rose smell, and are long-lasting as cut flowers. This rose blooms mid-season and repeats quickly and well. A vigorous shrub to 1.3m (4½ft), it has a spreading habit. To keep it in control, prune to inside-facing buds. The dark-green leaves are leathery and go to ground level on the stems. This rose is susceptible to mildew and black-spot, and needs winter protection in cold areas.

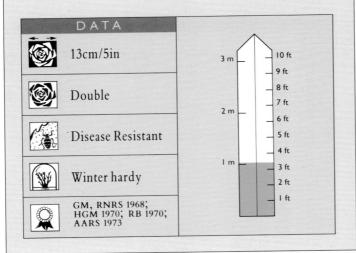

DATA	
13cm/5in	
Double	
Disease Resistant	
Winter hardy	
GM, RNRS 1968; HGM 1970; RB 1970; AARS 1973	

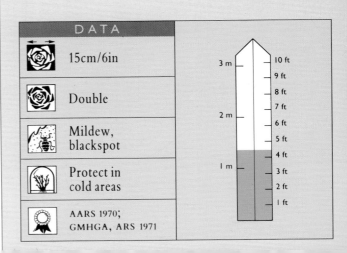

DATA	
15cm/6in	
Double	
Mildew, blackspot	
Protect in cold areas	
AARS 1970; GMHGA, ARS 1971	

'Garden Party'
~

Introduced in 1959, this is an offspring of 'Charlotte Armstrong' and 'Peace'. The 13–15cm (5–6in) double flowers are white with a touch of pink on the edges of the petals, and a high-centred form. Slightly fragrant, it blooms profusely in mid-season and repeats well. A vigorous shrub to 1.8m (6ft), it has an upright, bushy, well-branched habit. The medium-green leaves are semi-glossy. It is susceptible to mildew, but is otherwise disease resistant and winter hardy.

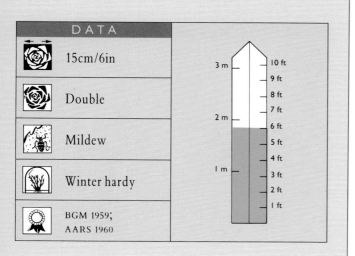

DATA	
15cm/6in	
Double	
Mildew	
Winter hardy	
BGM 1959; AARS 1960	

'Honor'
~

This rose was introduced as an award-winning trio with the grandiflora 'Love' and the floribunda 'Cherish' in 1980. The double, 10–13cm (4–5in) flowers are satiny-white with a high-centred form, maturing to a loose, open form. It is lightly fragrant, blooming well throughout the season, singly or in clusters. A vigorous shrub to 1.5m (5ft), it has an upright, well-balanced habit. The large leaves are dark green and leathery. It is disease resistant, but needs winter protection in cold areas.

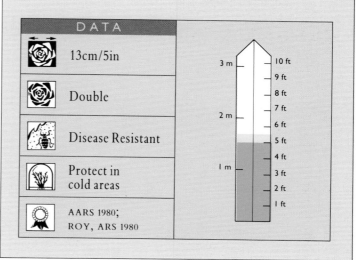

DATA	
13cm/5in	
Double	
Disease Resistant	
Protect in cold areas	
AARS 1980; ROY, ARS 1980	

'Medallion'
~

Introduced in 1973, this rose is best suited to a mild, cool climate. The 13–14cm (5–5½in) double flowers are an apricot blend to pink with yellow at the base of the petals. The form is loose, resembling a tulip. The fruity fragrance is reminiscent of ripe apples. This rose blooms profusely mid-season, and repeats well. A vigorous shrub to 1.5m (5ft), it has an upright, well-branched habit. The large leaves are bright green and leathery. It is a disease-resistant rose, but needs winter protection in cold areas.

DATA		
	14cm/5½in	
	Double	
	Disease Resistant	
	Protect in cold areas	
	AARS 1973	

'La France'
~

Introduced in 1867, this rose, considered to be the first hybrid tea, is still popular and available commercially today. The 10–11.5cm (4–4½in), very double and fragrant flowers are pale pink, with a brighter pink reverse. Borne in clusters, they have a high-centred form and are evenly petalled. This rose blooms profusely early to mid-season and repeats well. A moderately vigorous shrub growing to 1.2m (4ft), it has an upright, well-branched habit. The medium-green leaves are semi-glossy. It is disease resistant and winter hardy. There is a climbing form.

DATA		
	11.5cm/4½in	
	Very double	
	Disease Resistant	
	Winter hardy	
	No awards	

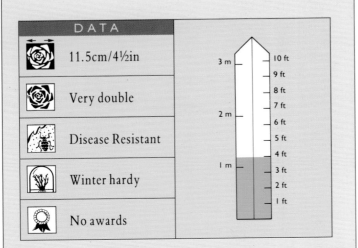

'Mister Lincoln'
~

Introduced in 1964, this rose is popular for its deep colour and its heavy, rich fragrance. The 13–15cm (5–6in), double flowers are dark red and appear velvety. The flowers are high-centred, opening to a cupped, well-filled form. This rose blooms well all season long; the colour is not affected by the weather. It is excellent as a cut flower and is a top exhibition rose. A vigorous shrub to 1.6m (5½ft), it has an upright, well-branched habit. The dark-green leaves are leathery and semi-glossy. It is disease resistant and winter hardy.

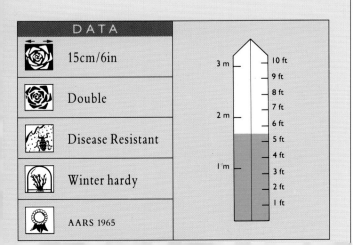

DATA	
15cm/6in	
Double	
Disease Resistant	
Winter hardy	
AARS 1965	

'Olympiad'
~

Introduced in 1984, this rose was named in honour of the Olympic Games. The 10–11.5cm (4–4½in), double flowers are medium red with a velvety appearance. The flowers are high-centred with a light fragrance. The colour holds well on the plant, and it is long-lasting as a cut flower. The flowers, borne singly or rarely in small clusters, bloom throughout the season. A vigorous shrub to 1.5m (5ft), it has a compact, upright habit. The medium-green, semi-glossy leaves are borne on very thorny canes.

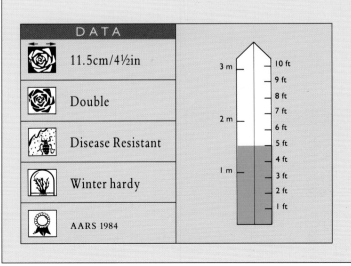

DATA	
11.5cm/4½in	
Double	
Disease Resistant	
Winter hardy	
AARS 1984	

'Oregold'
'MISS HARP'
~

Introduced in 1975, this rose has a true tea fragrance. The 11.5–14cm (4½–5½in), double flowers are a deep yellow that does not fade. The flowers have a classic high-centred form, maturing to a cup-shaped form. It is a good cut flower and an exhibition-quality rose. It blooms mid-season and is fairly recurrent. A moderately vigorous shrub to 1.2m (4ft), it has an upright, well-branched habit. The large leaves are dark green and glossy. It is susceptible to blackspot and mildew, but is otherwise disease resistant. It is marginally hardy and needs winter protection in cold areas.

'Paradise'
~

Introduced in 1978, this was the first lavender rose to win an AARS award. The 10–13cm (4–5in), double flowers are a mauve (lavender) blend with red. The flowers have a classic high-centred form, opening evenly. They are lightly fragrant and bloom well all season. A vigorous shrub to 1.3m (4½ft), this rose has an upright, well-branched habit. The dark-green leaves are thick and glossy. It is susceptible to mildew in cool, wet areas, but is otherwise disease resistant and winter hardy.

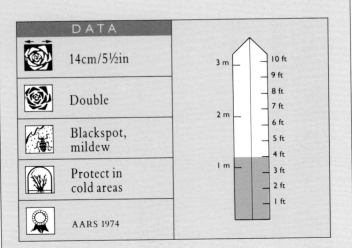

DATA	
14cm/5½in	
Double	
Blackspot, mildew	
Protect in cold areas	
AARS 1974	

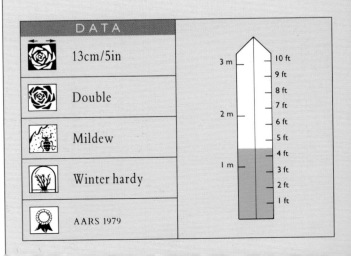

DATA	
13cm/5in	
Double	
Mildew	
Winter hardy	
AARS 1979	

'Pascali'
~

Introduced in 1963, this is the best bedder of all the white hybrid teas. The 9–11.5cm (3½–4½in) double flowers are creamy white and perfectly formed. In wet weather, the petals may spot with pink. This rose has a light fragrance, and blooms well all season. A very vigorous shrub to 1.2m (4ft), it has an upright, well-branched habit. The dark-green leaves are semi-glossy. 'Pascali' is disease resistant and winter hardy.

'Peace'
'MADAME ANTOINE MEILLAND', 'GLORIA DEI', 'GIOIA'
~

Introduced in 1945, this is the world's best-loved rose. The 13–15cm (5–6in) double flowers are a yellow blend with pink and cream. The classic high-centred form opens to divided or confused centres. 'Peace' has a very light fragrance. It does not bloom abundantly throughout the season, but the flowers it produces are almost perfect. A vigorous shrub to 1.8m (6ft), it has an upright and branching habit with stiff, moderately thorny canes. The large, dark-green leaves are glossy and leathery. It is disease resistant and winter hardy. There is a climbing form, which is considered to be the best of the hybrid tea climbers.

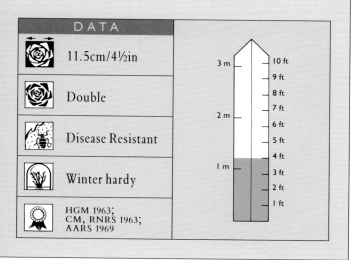

DATA	
11.5cm/4½in	
Double	
Disease Resistant	
Winter hardy	
HGM 1963; CM, RNRS 1963; AARS 1969	3 m — 10 ft / 9 ft / 8 ft / 7 ft / 2 m — 6 ft / 5 ft / 4 ft / 1 m — 3 ft / 2 ft / 1 ft

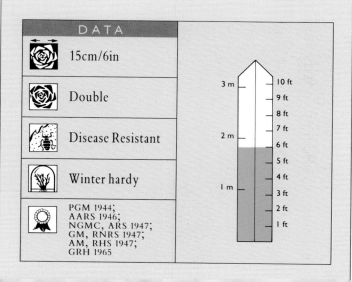

DATA	
15cm/6in	
Double	
Disease Resistant	
Winter hardy	
PGM 1944; AARS 1946; NGMC, ARS 1947; GM, RNRS 1947; AM, RHS 1947; GRH 1965	3 m — 10 ft / 9 ft / 8 ft / 2 m — 7 ft / 6 ft / 5 ft / 4 ft / 1 m — 3 ft / 2 ft / 1 ft

'Perfect Moment'
~

Introduced in 1991, this rose is uniquely coloured. The 10–13cm (4–5in), double flowers are yellow based with red tips. The buds open in a slow spiral to a high-centred flower. The flower lasts well on the plant and as a cut flower. It blooms mid-season and is recurrent. A vigorous shrub to 1.5m (5ft), it has an upright, well-branched form. the dark-green leaves are leathery. This rose is disease resistant and winter hardy.

'Perfume Delight'
~

Introduced in 1973, this rose has a strong, old-fashioned rose fragrance with a spicy overtone. The 10–13cm (4–5in), double flowers are a satiny, deep pink, and open to a cupped form. It blooms abundantly mid-season and is recurrent. A vigorous shrub to 1.3m (4½ft), it has an upright, bushy, well-branched habit. The large green leaves are medium green and leathery. This plant is susceptible to mildew and blackspot. It is also tender, and needs winter protection.

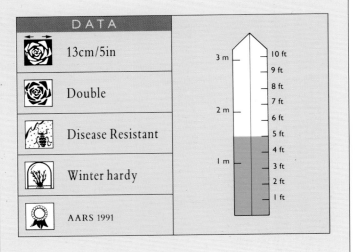

DATA	
13cm/5in	
Double	
Disease Resistant	
Winter hardy	
AARS 1991	

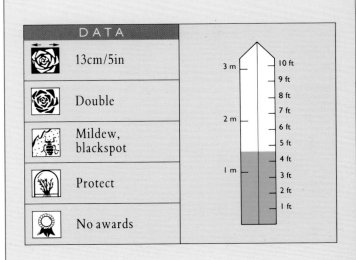

DATA	
13cm/5in	
Double	
Mildew, blackspot	
Protect	
No awards	

'Pink Peace'
~

Introduced in 1959, the name is confusing; this is not a sport of 'Peace', like 'Chicago Peace', but is a descendant of that great rose. The very double, 13–15cm (5–6in) flowers are medium to deep pink and somewhat cupped in form. It has an old-fashioned tea fragrance, and blooms abundantly throughout the season. A vigorous shrub to 1.3m (4½ft), it has an upright, bushy habit. The medium-green leaves are glossy and leathery. This rose is susceptible to rust and mildew, but is otherwise disease resistant and winter hardy.

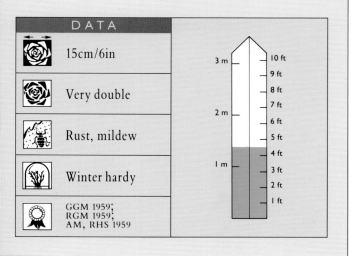

DATA		
15cm/6in	3 m	10 ft
		9 ft
Very double		8 ft
		7 ft
	2 m	6 ft
Rust, mildew		5 ft
		4 ft
Winter hardy	1 m	3 ft
		2 ft
GGM 1959; RGM 1959; AM, RHS 1959		1 ft

'Seashell'
~

Introduced in 1976, the name of this rose belies its deep colour. The 10–13cm (4–5in) flowers are an orange blend with pink, yellow and cream. The fragrant flowers bloom throughout the season, and are constantly changing colour with time. They have a high-centred form. Early flowers are borne singly; those later in the season are in clusters. A moderately vigorous shrub, it has an upright, well-branched habit. The dark-green leaves are glossy and thick, resembling holly. It is disease resistant and winter hardy.

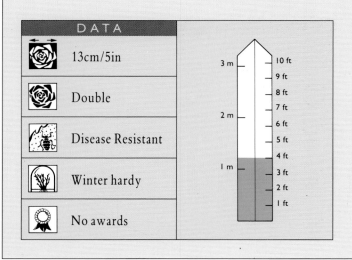

DATA		
13cm/5in	3 m	10 ft
		9 ft
Double		8 ft
		7 ft
	2 m	6 ft
Disease Resistant		5 ft
		4 ft
Winter hardy	1 m	3 ft
		2 ft
No awards		1 ft

'Sweet Surrender'
~

Introduced in 1983, this is a good cut flower. The 9–11.5cm (3½–4½in), double flowers are medium pink. They open almost flat in an evenly petalled form. Very fragrant, this rose blooms throughout the season. Growing 1–1.5m (3½–5ft) tall, it has an upright, compact habit. The large leaves are medium green and dull. This rose is tender, and needs winter protection.

'Tiffany'
~

Introduced in 1955, this is an ever-popular, fragrant rose. The 10–13cm (4–5in), double flowers are a pink blend with gold at the base of the petals. The flowers have a high-centred form. This rose blooms freely throughout the season, but does better in sun than in rain. The delightful rose essence is the trademark of this rose. It makes an excellent cut flower for its beauty, form and fragrance. A vigorous shrub to 1.3m (4½ft), it has an upright, bushy form. The dark-green leaves are glossy. 'Tiffany' is disease resistant and winter hardy. There is a climbing form.

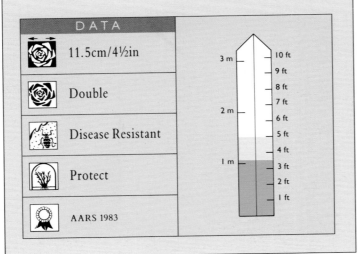

DATA	
11.5cm/4½in	3 m — 10 ft / 9 ft / 8 ft / 7 ft / 2 m — 6 ft / 5 ft / 4 ft / 1 m — 3 ft / 2 ft / 1 ft
Double	
Disease Resistant	
Protect	
AARS 1983	

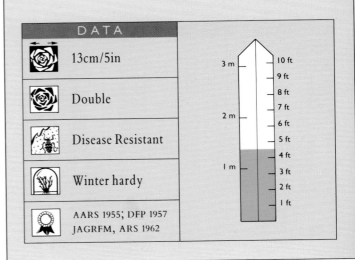

DATA	
13cm/5in	3 m — 10 ft / 9 ft / 8 ft / 7 ft / 2 m — 6 ft / 5 ft / 4 ft / 1 m — 3 ft / 2 ft / 1 ft
Double	
Disease Resistant	
Winter hardy	
AARS 1955; DFP 1957 JAGRFM, ARS 1962	

'Touch of Class'

~

Introduced in 1985, this is a descendant of 'Queen Elizabeth'. The 11.5–14cm (4½–5½in), double flowers are a warm pink blend with coral and cream. The flowers have the classic, high-centred form and are slightly fragrant. This rose blooms mid-season and is recurrent. A vigorous shrub to 1.5cm (5ft), it has an upright habit. The large leaves are dark green, glossy and abundant.

'Tropicana'
'SUPER STAR'

~

Introduced in Europe in 1960 and in the United States in 1962, this rose broke the colour barrier for orange, and is one of the top-selling roses of the century. The 11.5–13cm (4½–5in), double flowers are brilliant orange. They have a high-centred form, opening to cup-shaped flowers. This rose blooms abundantly throughout the season. It has a delightfully strong, fruity fragrance. A vigorous shrub, it has an upright, well-branched form. The dark-green leaves are glossy and leathery, borne on thorny canes. It is slightly susceptible to mildew, but is generally disease resistant and winter hardy. There is a climbing form.

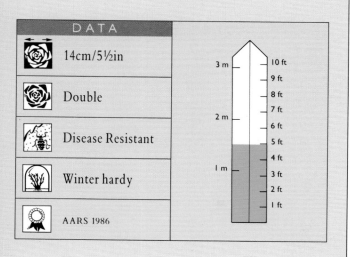

DATA	
	14cm/5½in
	Double
	Disease Resistant
	Winter hardy
	AARS 1986

3 m — 10 ft
9 ft
8 ft
2 m — 7 ft
6 ft
5 ft
4 ft
1 m — 3 ft
2 ft
1 ft

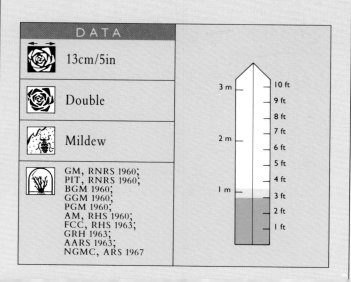

DATA	
	13cm/5in
	Double
	Mildew
	GM, RNRS 1960; PIT, RNRS 1960; BGM 1960; GGM 1960; PGM 1960; AM, RHS 1960; FCC, RHS 1963; GRH 1963; AARS 1963; NGMC, ARS 1967

3 m — 10 ft
9 ft
8 ft
2 m — 7 ft
6 ft
5 ft
4 ft
1 m — 3 ft
2 ft
1 ft

'Voodoo'
~

Introduced in 1985, this rose appears neon-orange in some lights. The double, 13–15cm (5–6in) flowers are an orange blend with yellow, peach and scarlet, fading to clear pink as they age. It blooms mid-season and is recurrent. The flowers are sweetly scented. A vigorous shrub to 1.6m (5½ft), it has an upright, well-branched habit. The dark-green leaves are semi-glossy. It is disease resistant, but needs winter protection in cold areas.

'White Delight'
~

Introduced in 1989, the 10–13cm (4–5in), double flowers are in fact an ivory-white colour blending to soft pink at the centre and the outer petals have a pale pink cast. It flowers freely and is recurrent. The flowers are borne singly on medium to long cutting stems. A vigorous shrub to 1.5m (5ft), it has an upright, well-branched habit. The dark-green leaves are glossy. It is disease resistant and winter hardy.

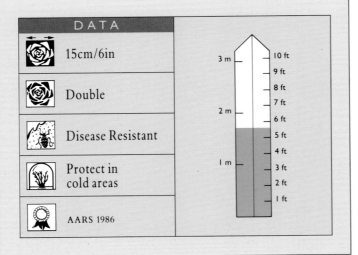

DATA	
15cm/6in	
Double	
Disease Resistant	
Protect in cold areas	
AARS 1986	

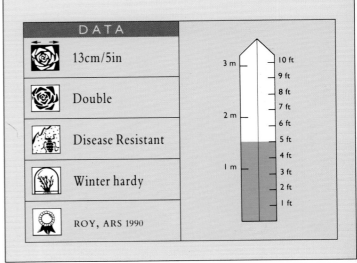

DATA	
13cm/5in	
Double	
Disease Resistant	
Winter hardy	
ROY, ARS 1990	

HYBRID TEA ROSES RESISTANT TO MILDEW

'Chicago Peace'
'Futura'
'Miss All-American Beauty'
'Mister Lincoln'
'Pascali'

'Peace'
'Pristine'
'Proud Land'
'Seashell'

HYBRID TEA ROSES RESISTANT TO BLACKSPOT

'Duet'
'Electron' ('Mullard Jubilee')
'Miss All-American Beauty'
'Mister Lincoln'

'Peace'
'Pink Peace'
'Pristine'
'Proud Land'

HIGHLY RECOMMENDED HYBRID TEA ROSES

RED
'Chrysler Imperial'
'Olympiad'
'Precious Platinum'
'Tropicana' ('Super Star')

WHITE
'Garden Party'
'Pascali'
'Pristine'
'White Knight'

MAUVE
'Lady X'

PINK
'Century Two'
'Dainty Bess'
'Electron' ('Mullard Jubilee')
'Miss All-American Beauty'

BLEND
'Granada'
'Maria Stern'
'Nantucket'
'Paradise'
'Peace'
'Swarthmore'

LEFT TO RIGHT 'Electron' is a highly recommended hybrid tea rose and resistant to blackspot; 'Proud Land' and 'Mister Lincoln' are resistant to blackspot and mildew.

FLORIBUNDA ROSES

DT Poulsen, a hybridizer from Denmark, can be credited with creating the first floribundas. His goal was to create a rose that would be hardy in the cold winters of northern Europe, floriferous, consistently recurrent, and require little or no special attention. A logical man, he felt that if he crossed a very hardy rose with a very attractive rose, the resultant rose would have the characteristics of both. He crossed the polyantha 'Orleans Rose' with the hybrid tea 'Red Star', and produced 'Else Poulsen' in 1924. He had created a new group of roses, which he called hybrid polyanthus; others called them Poulsen roses and it was not until the 1950s that these modern roses were finally called floribundas. Initially, the colours were limited to red and pink, and the roses lacked fragrance. Gene Boerner in the United States and Jack Harkness in Britain did much work with floribundas in the years following World War II, developing the characteristics so prized in hybrid tea roses: fragrance, a high-centred bloom, and a range of colours.

Today, floribundas rank second only to hybrid tea roses in their popularity. They fit into any landscape, formal or informal. Grow them into a hedge by planting two staggered rows 38cm (15in) apart, include them in a flower bed for contrast, or plant them by themselves for a splash of colour. Floribundas give a lot of colour for a little effort.

ABOVE Multiple blooms are a feature of floribunda roses, such as 'Bahia', providing an unmistakable splash of colour.
~

'Apricot Nectar'
~

Introduced in 1965, this is a vigorous bushy rose growing to 1.2m (4ft). The 10–11.5cm (4–4½in) flowers are pinkish-apricot and yellow at the base. The fragrant, double flowers are found singly and in clusters, freely blooming from mid-season on. This rose's pastel colour is unique among floribundas. It has smooth canes with few thorns, and medium-green leaves. It is disease resistant and very winter hardy.

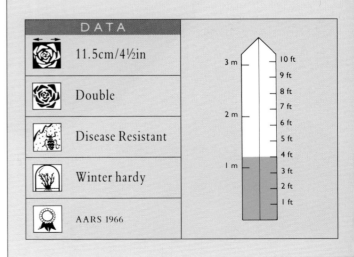

DATA	
11.5cm/4½in	
Double	
Disease Resistant	
Winter hardy	
AARS 1966	

'Bahia'

~

This rose, introduced in 1974, is a vigorous, upright shrub to 1m (3½ft). The coral buds open to 6–10cm (2½–4in) orange blend double flowers in small clusters. A profuse bloomer, with a spicy fragrance, it blooms freely throughout the season. The leaves are dark green and glossy. It is disease resistant and winter hardy.

'Betty Prior'

~

Although it was introduced in 1935, this rose is still popular today. At first glance this single rose looks more like a species or species hybrid than a floribunda. With its proliferation of mildly fragrant, medium to deep-pink flowers, it resembles a tiny flowering dogwood. The cupped, five-petal flowers bloom in clusters. It blooms profusely in mid-season and repeats well. Growing up to 2.1m (7ft) with an upright bushy habit, it has medium-green leaves. It is disease resistant and winter hardy.

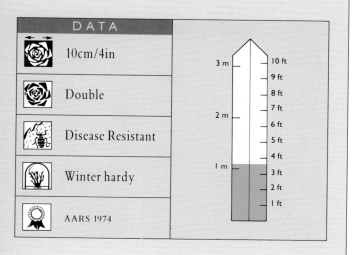

DATA	
10cm/4in	
Double	
Disease Resistant	
Winter hardy	
AARS 1974	

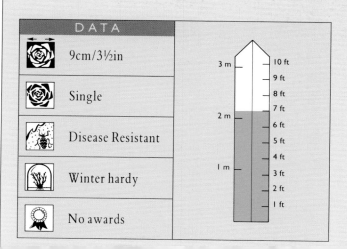

DATA	
9cm/3½in	
Single	
Disease Resistant	
Winter hardy	
No awards	

'Cathedral'

'COVENTRY CATHEDRAL'

~

Introduced in 1975, this rose is considered an apricot blend; the buds are apricot, but the 7.5–9cm (3–3½in) high-centred double flowers are a bright scarlet-salmon blending to pale apricot or cream. It has a sweet fragrance and cuts well. Blooming mid-season, the flowers are recurrent. It grows to 1.2m (4ft) with an upright bushy habit and has dark-green, glossy leaves. It is disease resistant and winter hardy.

'Charisma'

~

Introduced in 1977, it grows to 1m (3½ft) with an upright, well-branched, spreading habit. The 6–7.5cm (2½–3in) double flowers are a red and yellow blend, with the red becoming more prominent as the flower matures. It blooms mid-season, repeating well. The leaves are leathery green. It is disease resistant and winter hardy.

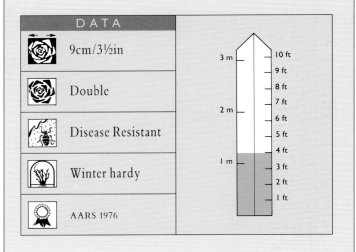

DATA	
9cm/3½in	
Double	
Disease Resistant	
Winter hardy	
AARS 1976	

3 m — 10 ft / 9 ft / 8 ft / 7 ft
2 m — 6 ft / 5 ft / 4 ft
1 m — 3 ft / 2 ft / 1 ft

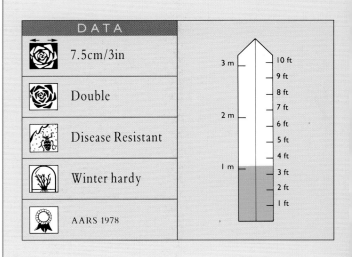

DATA	
7.5cm/3in	
Double	
Disease Resistant	
Winter hardy	
AARS 1978	

3 m — 10 ft / 9 ft / 8 ft / 7 ft
2 m — 6 ft / 5 ft / 4 ft
1 m — 3 ft / 2 ft / 1 ft

'Cherish'
~

Introduced in 1980, it has high-centred, medium-pink flowers which are long-lasting when cut. The double flowers, borne in clusters, are 7.5–10cm (3–4in) wide. There is an interesting cinnamon overtone to the fragrance. An early bloomer, it flowers prolifically throughout the season. It is a vigorous shrub, growing to 1.2m (4ft) with a handsome symmetrical habit. The leaves are deep green and glossy. It is disease resistant and winter hardy.

'Class Act'
~

Introduced in 1989, this rose is easy to grow. A vigorous plant, growing to 1.2m (4ft), it blooms all season long. The cream-coloured buds open to large (10cm/4in), double, white blossoms, tinged yellow at the base of the petals, revealing golden stamens at the centre. It has an upright, bushy habit. The leaves are dark green and glossy. It is disease resistant and winter hardy.

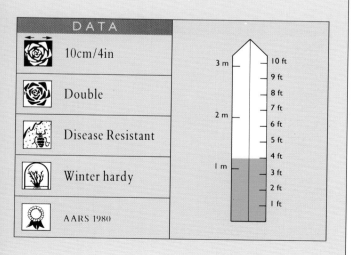

DATA	
10cm/4in	
Double	
Disease Resistant	
Winter hardy	
AARS 1980	

3 m — 10 ft
9 ft
8 ft
2 m — 7 ft
6 ft
5 ft
4 ft
1 m — 3 ft
2 ft
1 ft

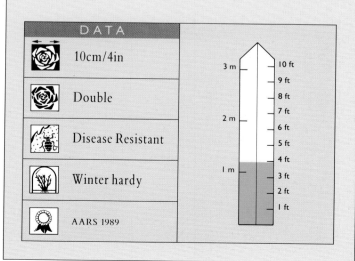

DATA	
10cm/4in	
Double	
Disease Resistant	
Winter hardy	
AARS 1989	

3 m — 10 ft
9 ft
8 ft
2 m — 7 ft
6 ft
5 ft
4 ft
1 m — 3 ft
2 ft
1 ft

'Escapade'

~

Introduced in 1967, the flowers are technically semi-double as they have 12 petals, but they bear more resemblance to single flowers. It is a prolific bloomer with 7.5cm (3in) rosy-mauve flowers with white centres that open fully to show the golden stamens. It blooms mid-season and is recurrent. The fragrance is slightly musky but pleasant. This bushy, well-branched rose grows to 90cm (3ft). The leaves are abundant, light green and glossy. It is disease resistant and winter hardy.

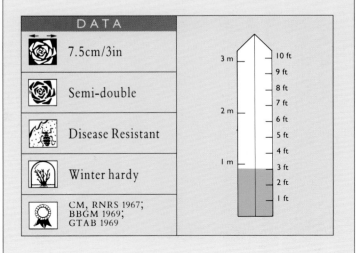

DATA	
🌹	7.5cm/3in
🌹	Semi-double
🐜	Disease Resistant
🌿	Winter hardy
🏅	CM, RNRS 1967; BBGM 1969; GTAB 1969

'Europeana'

~

Introduced in 1963, this top-rated dark-red rose flowers abundantly in mid-season and has good repeat bloom. The flowers, produced in large clusters, are lightly fragrant, semi-double, and cupped in form. The clusters need support to keep them from breaking during heavy rain. It is a bushy, spreading, vigorous shrub that grows up to 90cm (3ft) tall. Young leaves are coppery, maturing to a glossy bronze-green. It is prone to mildew in some areas, but is winter hardy.

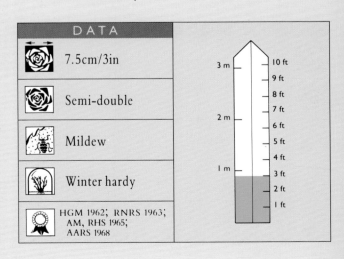

DATA	
🌹	7.5cm/3in
🌹	Semi-double
🐜	Mildew
🌿	Winter hardy
🏅	HGM 1962; RNRS 1963; AM, RHS 1965; AARS 1968

'Evening Star'
~

Introduced in 1974, this is sold in Europe as a hybrid tea, and in the United States as a floribunda. It is one of a series of crosses of hybrid teas with floribundas, which may be a future trend for roses. An upright, vigorous bush, it is a profuse mid-season bloomer with fair repeat bloom. The buds are pointed, opening to a high-centred, double, white flower with a flush of yellow at the base. It blooms singly or in small clusters and the flowers are long lasting. Growing to 1m (3½ft) tall, it has large, dark-green leathery leaves. It is disease resistant but tender.

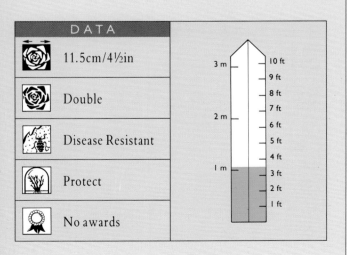

DATA	
11.5cm/4½in	
Double	
Disease Resistant	
Protect	
No awards	

'Fashion'
~

Introduced in 1948, this rose is ever popular. It is a vigorous, upright, bushy plant to 1.3m (4½ft). The peach blend flowers are double, 7.5–9cm (3–3½in) wide. It was one of the first floribundas to have the high-centred flower typical of the hybrid tea. It blooms mid-season singly or in small clusters. It repeats well and the colour does not fade. The medium-green leaves are borne on thorny canes. It is disease resistant and winter hardy.

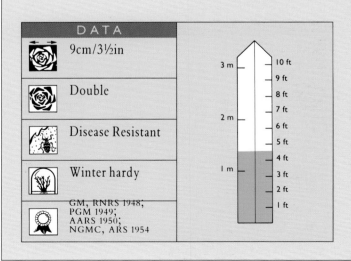

DATA	
9cm/3½in	
Double	
Disease Resistant	
Winter hardy	
GM, RNRS 1948; PGM 1949; AARS 1950; NGMC, ARS 1954	

'First Edition'
~

Introduced in 1977, this is a good all-round landscape rose. It is a vigorous, well-branched, upright shrub that grows to 1.2m (4ft). The lightly-scented, 6–7.5cm (2½–3in), double flowers are orange blended with yellow, coral, pink and red, borne singly and in clusters. It blooms mid-season and is fairly recurrent. It is good as a cut flower and is a top exhibition rose. The light-green leaves are large and glossy. It is disease resistant, but needs winter protection in cold areas.

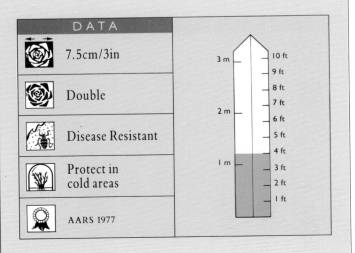

DATA	
7.5cm/3in	
Double	3 m — 10 ft / 9 ft / 8 ft / 7 ft
Disease Resistant	2 m — 6 ft / 5 ft / 4 ft
Protect in cold areas	1 m — 3 ft / 2 ft / 1 ft
AARS 1977	

'French Lace'
~

Introduced in 1980, this is an upright plant with a well-branched, bushy habit growing to 1m (3½ft). The lightly fragrant, white flowers are 9–10cm (3½–4in), double, and high-centred. It blooms mid-season and is recurrent. The medium-green leaves are semi-glossy on thorny stems. It is disease resistant and winter hardy.

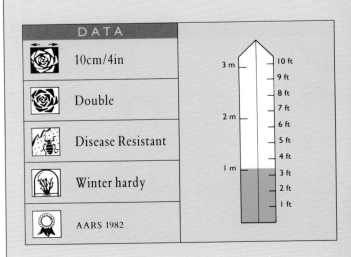

DATA	
10cm/4in	
Double	3 m — 10 ft / 9 ft / 8 ft / 7 ft
Disease Resistant	2 m — 6 ft / 5 ft / 4 ft
Winter hardy	1 m — 3 ft / 2 ft / 1 ft
AARS 1982	

'Gene Boerner'

~

This rose, introduced in 1969, is named for the hybridizer who has done remarkable work in the development of floribundas. It is tall for a floribunda, growing to 1.5m (5ft), with an upright, narrow habit. Very free-flowering, it blooms mid-season with an excellent repeat bloom. The 7.5–9cm (3–3½in), double flowers are uniformly pink, and high-centred. The flowers are borne singly or in clusters on strong long stems. The medium-green leaves are semi-glossy on somewhat thorny canes. It is disease resistant and winter hardy.

'Gingersnap'

~

Introduced in 1978, this floribunda has a light fruity fragrance. It is a bushy, upright plant, growing to 1m (3½ft). The 10–11.5cm (4–4½in) double flowers are orange, blending to red at the edges and yellow at the base. It blooms early to mid-season, but is not reliably recurrent. The ruffled-edged flowers are borne singly or in clusters. The foliage is deep green, glossy and abundant. A vigorous plant, it is disease resistant, but somewhat tender, needing winter protection in colder areas.

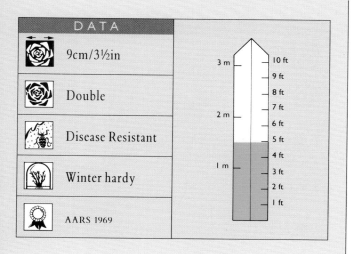

DATA	
9cm/3½in	
Double	
Disease Resistant	
Winter hardy	
AARS 1969	

DATA	
11.5cm/4½in	
Double	
Disease Resistant	
Protect in cold areas	
No awards	

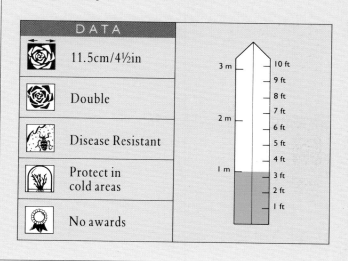

'Iceberg'
'SCHNEEWITTCHEN', 'FEE DES NEIGES'
~

Introduced in 1958, this is an ideal rose for a hedge. It is an upright, bushy, 1.2m (4ft) plant that produces many shoots creating a very graceful shrub. The 7.5cm (3in), double, white flowers are high-centred, opening to a cupped form. They are borne in clusters and are fragrant. Blooming early to mid-season, it continues to flower throughout the season. The light-green leaves are semi-glossy, on nearly thornless canes. It is susceptible to blackspot, but is very winter hardy.

'Impatient'
~

Introduced in 1984, the blossoms are characteristic of a hybrid tea. The double orange-red flowers are 7.5cm (3in) wide with a yellow base. The blooms are borne singly and in small clusters. It flowers mid-season and is recurrent. An upright shrub, growing to 1m (3½ft), it is vigorous and well-branched. The foliage is dark green and semi-glossy on very thorny canes. It is disease resistant and winter hardy.

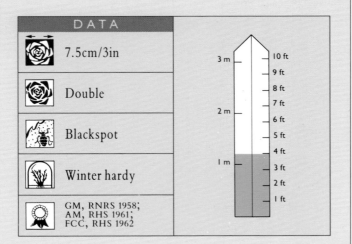

DATA	
	7.5cm/3in
	Double
	Blackspot
	Winter hardy
	GM, RNRS 1958; AM, RHS 1961; FCC, RHS 1962

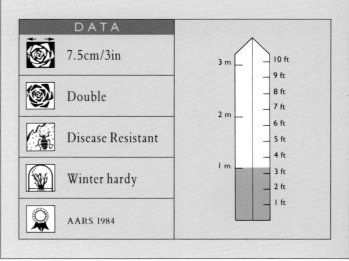

DATA	
	7.5cm/3in
	Double
	Disease Resistant
	Winter hardy
	AARS 1984

'Marina'

~

Introduced in Europe in 1974 and in the United States in 1980, this floribunda is often grown as a greenhouse rose. It is a very good cut flower. A vigorous shrub growing to 1m (3½ft), it has a very bushy, upright habit. The 6–7.5cm (2½–3in) double flowers are an orange blend, with red and gold. The blooms are high-centred, borne in clusters on long stems. The dark-green, glossy leaves are abundant. It is disease resistant and winter hardy.

'Pleasure'

~

Introduced in 1989, this floribunda has a vigorous upright habit, growing to 1m (3½ft). The coral pink buds slowly spiral open to 6–9cm (2½–3½in) bright coral-pink blossoms that have a hint of yellow at the base of the petals. The slightly ruffled flowers are produced in abundance throughout the growing season. It is disease resistant and winter hardy.

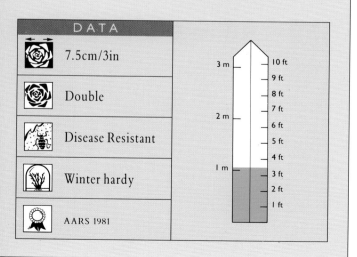

DATA	
	7.5cm/3in
	Double
	Disease Resistant
	Winter hardy
	AARS 1981

3 m — 10 ft
9 ft
8 ft
7 ft
2 m — 6 ft
5 ft
4 ft
1 m — 3 ft
2 ft
1 ft

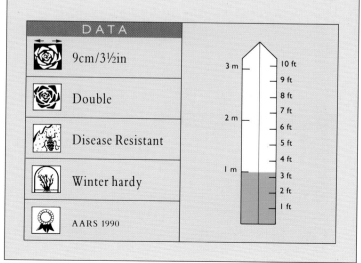

DATA	
	9cm/3½in
	Double
	Disease Resistant
	Winter hardy
	AARS 1990

3 m — 10 ft
9 ft
8 ft
7 ft
2 m — 6 ft
5 ft
4 ft
1 m — 3 ft
2 ft
1 ft

'Redgold'
'ROUGE ET OR'
~

Introduced in 1966, this rose must be grown in full sun to develop its unique coloration. It is a vigorous, well-branched, upright shrub to 1m (3½ft). The double, 6–7.5cm (2½–3in), yellow blend flowers are tipped in bold red and have a light fruity fragrance. The flowers are high-centred, opening to a cup shape, and are borne singly and in clusters. It blooms mid-season with a fair repeat bloom. The canes are very thorny, with sparse medium-green leaves. It is disease resistant and winter hardy.

DATA	
7.5cm/3in	
Double	
Disease Resistant	
Winter hardy	
CM, RNRS 1966; AARS 1971	

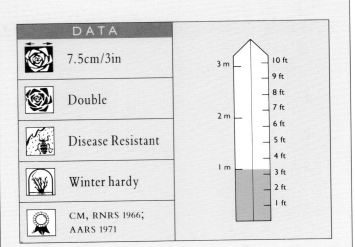

'Sarabande'
~

Introduced in 1957, this showy rose is adaptable, but performs best in areas with cool summers. The 6cm (2½in) bright orange-red flowers are semi-double with a cupped to flat form, opening to reveal bright-yellow stamens. The colour does not quickly fade. It blooms profusely in large clusters in mid-season and gives a very good repeat bloom. The fragrance is light, with spicy tones. Growing to 75cm (2½ft), with a vigorous bushy habit, it is ideal as a bedding plant. The medium-green leaves are semi-glossy on fairly thorny stems. It is disease resistant and winter hardy.

DATA	
6cm/2½in	
Semi-double	
Disease Resistant	
Winter hardy	
BGM 1957; GGM 1957; RGM 1957; PGM 1958; AARS 1960	

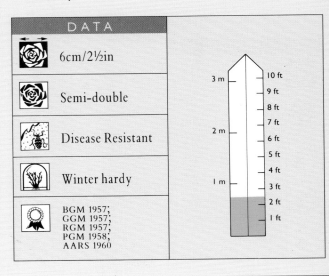

'Showbiz'

'INGRID WIEBULL', 'BERNHARD DANEKE ROSE'

~

Introduced in 1981, this rose is vigorous with upright spreading habit, growing to 90cm (3ft). The 6–7.5cm (2½–3in) medium-red flowers are double, with open cupped form. The petals are ruffled. Slightly fragrant, this rose blooms well all season with the flowers in clusters. The dark-green leaves are glossy. It is disease resistant and winter hardy.

DATA		
7.5cm/3in		3 m — 10 ft / 9 ft / 8 ft
Double		2 m — 7 ft / 6 ft / 5 ft
Disease Resistant		4 ft
Winter hardy		1 m — 3 ft / 2 ft / 1 ft
AARS 1985		

FLORIBUNDA AND GRANDIFLORA ROSES RESISTANT TO BLACKSPOT

'Angel Face'
'Carousel'
'Europeana'
'First Edition'
'Gene Boerner'
'Ivory Fashion'

'Montezuma'
'Prominent' ('Korp')
'Queen Elizabeth'
'Razzle Dazzle'
'Sonia' ('Sweet Promise')

HIGHLY RECOMMENDED FLORIBUNDA ROSES

RED
'Europeana'
'Impatient'
'Lichterloh'
'Showbiz'

PINK
'Cherish'
'Gene Boerner'
'Sexy Rexy'
'Simplicity'

YELLOW
'Sunsprite' ('Korresia')

MAUVE
'Escapade'

WHITE
'Evening Star'
'Iceberg'
'Ivory Fashion'

BLEND
'Anabell'
'Angel Face'
'Apricot Nectar'
'Sea Pearl'
'Summer Fashion'

FLORIBUNDA AND GRANDIFLORA ROSES RESISTANT TO MILDEW

'Queen Elizabeth'
'Razzle Dazzle'
'Rose Parade'
'Sarabande'
'Saratoga'

'Cathedral'
'Charisma'
'Evening Star'
'First Edition'
'Prominent ('Korp')

GRANDIFLORA OR FLORIBUNDA HYBRID-TEA TYPE ROSES

Grandifloras are the newest class of rose, created in the United States in 1954 for the rose 'Queen Elizabeth'. The hybrid tea 'Charlotte Armstrong' was the seed parent, with the floribunda 'Floradora' the pollen parent. By Act of Parliament, Queen Elizabeth II gave permission to use her name for this stately rose.

Most grandifloras are the results of crosses with 'Queen Elizabeth' or other offspring of 'Charlotte Armstrong' and 'Floradora'. In the United States, the results of some of these crosses are not considered grandifloras, and are instead classified in the floribunda subclass, 'floribunda, hybrid-tea type'. The British have not recognized grandiflora as a separate class, and place all such roses in that same floribunda subclass.

Grandifloras are crosses between hybrid teas and floribundas, with the resulting roses having the best characteristics of both types. They bloom continuously through the growing season. They are floriferous, with an abundance of 7.5–13cm (3–5in) double flowers, borne singly or in clusters. The stems are longer than those of floribundas. Unfortunately, they did not inherit the floribunda's hardiness, and do not survive cold winters without good protection. The resemblance to hybrid teas is evident in the buds, flowers, leaves and thorns. The range of colours is extensive, but there are no lavenders and few bicolours. Oddly, grandifloras are taller than either of their parents, growing from 90 to 180cm (3 to 6ft) or taller. 'Queen Elizabeth' is a statuesque 210cm (7ft).

When incorporating grandifloras in the garden, make good use of their height. They are excellent as a background plant, whether in a rose garden or perennial border. They can be used to create good hedges. With their long stems, even on the clustered blooms, they are impressive as cut flowers.

ABOVE *Unsurpassed in beauty, colour, stature, or quality and quantity of bloom, 'Queen Elizabeth' reigns supreme among the grandifloras.*
~

'Aquarius'
~

Introduced in 1971, this grandiflora is exceptionally long-lasting as a cut flower. The 9–11cm (3½–4½in), double flowers are a medium bright-pink blend with cream. The flower form is high-centred and evenly petalled. It blooms well throughout the season, with a mild fragrance. The flowers hold well even in the heat of the summer. Growing to 1.5m (5ft), this rose has a vigorous, upright bushy habit. The large leaves are reddish-green. 'Aquarius' is exceptionally disease resistant and winter hardy.

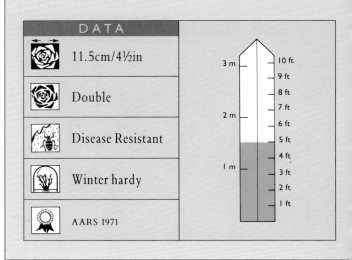

DATA	
🌹	11.5cm/4½in
🌹	Double
🐜	Disease Resistant
🌿	Winter hardy
🏅	AARS 1971

3 m — 10 ft / 9 ft / 8 ft
2 m — 7 ft / 6 ft / 5 ft
1 m — 4 ft / 3 ft / 2 ft / 1 ft

'Arizona'
~

Introduced in 1975, this is an intensely fragrant rose. The 10–11.5cm (4–4½) double flowers are an orange blend with pink and bronze. This rose blooms throughout the season with non-fading flowers borne singly or in clusters. It grows to 1.5m (5ft) with long, slender, thorny canes. The bronze-green leaves are leathery and semi-glossy. It is disease resistant, but needs winter protection.

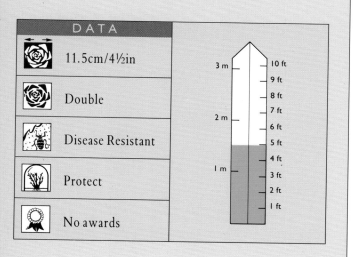

DATA	
11.5cm/4½in	
Double	
Disease Resistant	
Protect	
No awards	

'Gold Medal'
~

Introduced in 1982, this is a handsomely coloured rose. The 9cm (3½in), double flowers are deep yellow, brushed with red at the edges. The high-centred flowers have a unique fruity, tea-like fragrance. Blooms are borne singly or in clusters throughout the season. Growing 1.3–1.6m (4½–5½ft) tall, it is vigorous with an upright bushy habit. The dark-green leaves are semi-glossy. It is susceptible to blackspot and only marginally hardy.

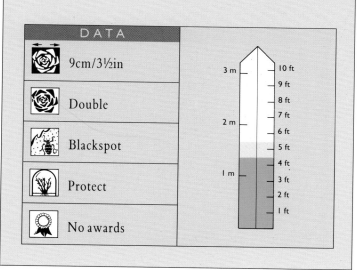

DATA	
9cm/3½in	
Double	
Blackspot	
Protect	
No awards	

'Love'
~

This was introduced in 1980, with 'Honor', a hybrid tea, and 'Cherish', a floribunda. The 9cm (3½in) double flowers are striking – red with white reverse, and have the high-centred form typical of hybrid teas, developing into a cupped form with a confused centre. The mildly spicy blooms continue throughout the season. Growing 90–105cm (3–3½ft) it has an upright, symmetrical, sparsely branched habit. The leaves are medium green, borne on very thorny canes. It is disease resistant and winter hardy.

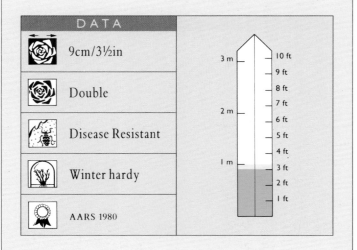

DATA	
9cm/3½in	
Double	
Disease Resistant	
Winter hardy	
AARS 1980	

'New Year'
~

Introduced in 1987, this is a compact plant with sturdy stems. The 7.5–9cm (3–3½) double flowers are a unique orange blend ith peach and yellow. The flowers have a high-centred form, and last well when cut. It blooms throughout the season. Growing to 1m (3½ft), this rose is vigorous with a compact, dense habit. It is disease resistant and winter hardy.

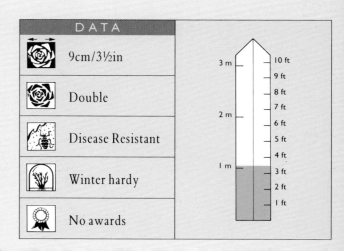

DATA	
9cm/3½in	
Double	
Disease Resistant	
Winter hardy	
No awards	

'Prominent'
'KORP'
~

Introduced in 1971, this is a striking rose to put in the garden. The 9cm (3½in) double flowers are orange-red and high-centred. As it opens to cupped form, the petals recurve, but the colour does not fade. It blooms well all season with a light, fruity fragrance. Growing 1–1.3m (3½–4½ft) tall, it has an upright, well-branched habit with thorny canes. The dark-green leaves are leathery. It is disease resistant and winter hardy.

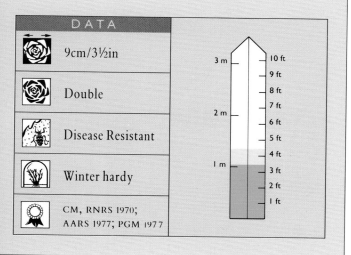

DATA	
9cm/3½in	
Double	
Disease Resistant	
Winter hardy	
CM, RNRS 1970; AARS 1977; PGM 1977	

'Queen Elizabeth'
~

This grandiflora has been one of the world's most popular roses since its introduction in 1954. The 9–10cm (3½–4in), double flowers are clear medium-pink, and have a high-centred form opening to a cupped form. It has a mild fragrance, blooming abundantly in mid-season, repeating very well. The flowers are borne singly or in clusters on long, almost thornless stems. A tall rose, growing from 1.5–2.1m (5–7ft), it is very vigorous with an upright, bushy habit. The foliage is deep green and glossy. This rose is disease resistant and winter hardy.

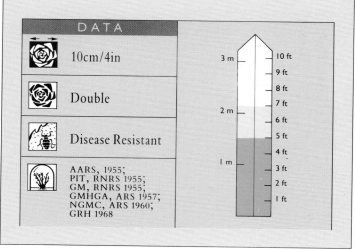

DATA	
10cm/4in	
Double	
Disease Resistant	
AARS, 1955; PIT, RNRS 1955; GM, RNRS 1955; GMHGA, ARS 1957; NGMC, ARS 1960; GRH 1968	

'Shining Hour'
~

Introduced in 1991, this rose is extremely floriferous. The 10–13cm (4–5in) double flowers have the classic high-centred form. A bright sunny yellow, it blooms mid-season and repeats well. A vigorous shrub to 1.3m (4½ft), it has an upright, dense habit. The medium-green leaves are glossy. It is disease resistant and winter hardy.

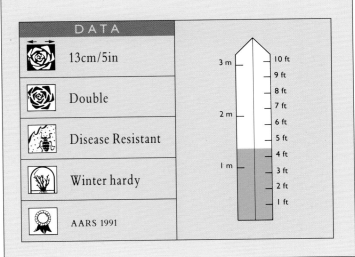

DATA	
🌹	13cm/5in
🌹	Double
🐞	Disease Resistant
🌿	Winter hardy
🏵	AARS 1991

'Sundowner'
~

Introduced in 1978, the colour of this rose matches its name. The 10cm (4in) double flowers are an orange blend with apricot and gold. The high-centred blooms open to cupped form. It blooms throughout the season, with flowers borne singly on long stems; late in the season the blooms may be clustered. The fragrance is strong and spicy. Growing to 1.3–1.6m (4½–5½ft), it is vigorous with an upright, well-balanced habit. It is prone to mildew in cool, damp areas, but is otherwise disease resistant and winter hardy.

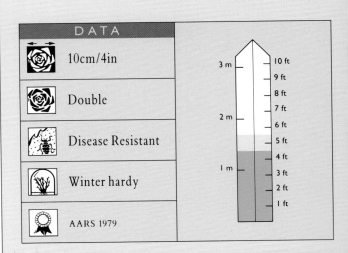

DATA	
🌹	10cm/4in
🌹	Double
🐞	Disease Resistant
🌿	Winter hardy
🏵	AARS 1979

'Tournament of Roses'
~

Introduced in 1989, this rose is named after the annual Tournament of Roses parade, held on New Year's Day in Pasadena, California. The 9cm (3½in) double flowers are coral-pink. As the petals open, the colour lightens, more quickly on the top than the reverse, giving a bicolour effect to the mature flower. It blooms throughout the season. Growing to 1.5m (5ft), it has an upright, bushy habit. The leaves are dark and glossy. It is disease resistant and winter hardy.

'White Lightnin''
~

Introduced in 1980, this grandiflora has a strong citrus fragrance, The 9–10cm (3½–4in) double flowers are white, delicately edged in pink. It opens to cupped form with gently scalloped petals. Blooming throughout the season, the flowers are borne in clusters. A vigorous shrub to 1.3m (4½ft), it has an upright bushy habit. The deep-green leaves are glossy on moderately thorny canes. It is disease resistant and winter hardy.

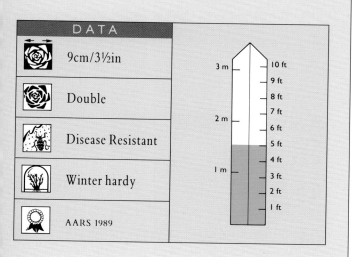

DATA	
9cm/3½in	
Double	
Disease Resistant	
Winter hardy	
AARS 1989	

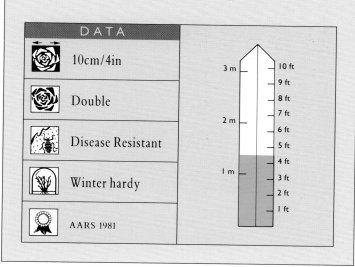

DATA	
10cm/4in	
Double	
Disease Resistant	
Winter hardy	
AARS 1981	

CLIMBING ROSES

Roses are not vines and do not have tendrils with which to attach themselves. On their own, roses would not climb. With a bit of help from humans to provide support in the form of a trellis, wall, pillar, arbour or the like, and a strong material to attach the rose to the support, roses do climb – magnificently. The 'ideal' cottage in the country brings to mind a house on a narrow lane with a white-painted fence and a white arbour over the entrance gate covered with fragrant red roses. The most difficult part of growing climbers is placing them and securing them to the support. After that, they are on their own; even pruning is kept to a minimum with climbers.

Climbers do not have to be supported, they can trail along the ground and can be particularly effective trailing down a hillside. Not only do they provide beauty to an area that can be awkward to plant, they also help to hold the soil and prevent erosion.

There are a number of groups of roses which are considered climbers, including climbing hybrid teas, large-flowered climbers, hybrid wichuraiana climbers, hybrid bracteatas, hybrid giganteas, kordesii climbers and ramblers. The largest group by far is the large-flowered climbers. They have 5–15cm (2–6in) flowers on strong flexible canes that grow from 1.8m–4.5m (6–15ft) long. The range of colour is wide; some are recurrent bloomers, others bloom but once.

Pillar roses are a subclass of the large-flowered climbers that have shorter (1.5–3m/5–10ft), but stiffer canes, so they tend to be more upright even without support. They are often planted by posts or pillars for support to keep them from snapping in high winds, hence their name.

The rambler is perhaps best known of the climbers. The supple canes can grow from 3–6m (10–20ft) in a year. They have dense clusters of small 5cm (2in) flowers in late spring or early summer on one-year-old canes. Most are not recurrent. The colours are generally limited to deep red, pink, white and peachy yellow.

The climbing forms of hybrid teas, polyanthas, floribundas, grandifloras and miniatures originated as sports from the normal plants. They are similar to the original plant, but have longer canes, fewer blooms and are less hardy.

ABOVE *Climbers are particularly attractive if trained up the side of the house or around a doorway or porch.*
~

'*America*'
~

A large flowered climber, introduced in 1976, it grows from 2.7–3.6m (9–12ft) tall with an upright, vigorous habit. The 9–11.5cm (3½–4½in) salmon-coral flowers are double, evenly petalled and high centred. This rose blooms mid-season and is fairly recurrent. It is disease resistant and winter hardy.

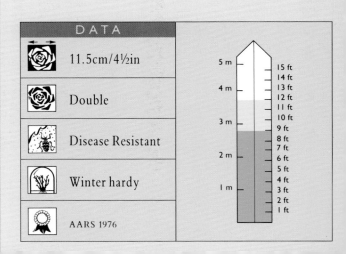

DATA	
11.5cm/4½in	
Double	
Disease Resistant	
Winter hardy	
AARS 1976	

5 m   15 ft / 14 ft / 13 ft / 12 ft / 11 ft
4 m
3 m   10 ft / 9 ft
  8 ft / 7 ft / 6 ft
2 m   5 ft
  4 ft / 3 ft
1 m   2 ft / 1 ft

'Don Juan'
~

Introduced in 1958, this is a striking large-flowered climber with dark-red, velvety, 11.5–13cm (4½–5in), flowers. It grows to 3m (10ft) tall. The flowers are very fragrant, double with a high centre, and recurrent. The foliage is dark green and leathery. A vigorous upright plant, this rose is disease resistant, but not consistently winter hardy.

'Dorothy Perkins'
~

Introduced in 1901, this rambler was so popular for many years that some considered it to be overplanted. Other plants are now in vogue, but this rose still has a loyal following. It can even be found still growing, although neglected, in areas where it was once cultivated. Growing to 3–3.6m (10–12ft), it blooms late in the season, and is neither fragrant nor recurrent. The flowers are small (2cm/¾in) and double or semi-double, borne in clusters. They are bright medium pink with a slight blue tone. The leaves are small, glossy and dark green. This rose is susceptible to mildew, so needs to be trained so that it gets optimal air circulation. Do not grow it against a wall. It is winter hardy.

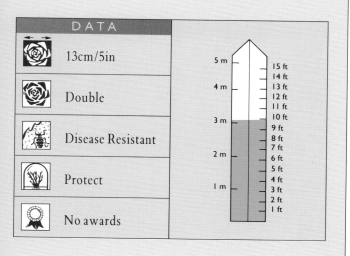

DATA	
13cm/5in	
Double	
Disease Resistant	
Protect	
No awards	

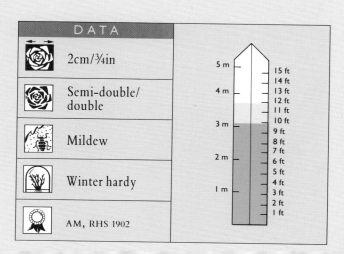

DATA	
2cm/¾in	
Semi-double/ double	
Mildew	
Winter hardy	
AM, RHS 1902	

'Golden Showers'
~

An award-winning large flowered climber, introduced in 1956. It grows to 1.8–3m (6–10ft) tall, and is extremely floriferous. The 9–10cm (3½–4in) golden-yellow flowers are double, fragrant and cupped. The flowers open flat, with the golden colour fading to cream as they mature. It is free-flowering throughout the season. Glossy, dark-green leaves are borne on thorny canes. This rose is disease resistant and winter hardy in all but the coldest areas.

'Gladiator'
~

Introduced in 1955, this large-flowered climber has 10–13cm (4–5in) medium-red flowers on canes that grow to 3.6m (12ft). It blooms continuously from mid-season with fragrant, double blossoms that fade in colour as they mature. The foliage is dark green and leathery. This rose is disease resistant, but not consistently winter hardy.

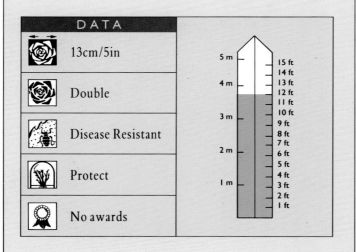

DATA	
13cm/5in	
Double	
Disease Resistant	
Protect	
No awards	

5 m — 15 ft
— 14 ft
4 m — 13 ft
— 12 ft
— 11 ft
3 m — 10 ft
— 9 ft
— 8 ft
— 7 ft
2 m — 6 ft
— 5 ft
— 4 ft
1 m — 3 ft
— 2 ft
— 1 ft

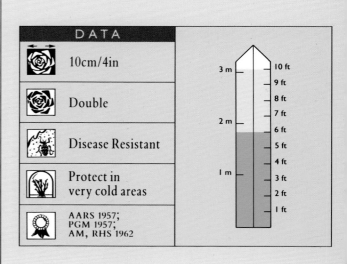

DATA	
10cm/4in	
Double	
Disease Resistant	
Protect in very cold areas	
AARS 1957; PGM 1957; AM, RHS 1962	

3 m — 10 ft
— 9 ft
— 8 ft
— 7 ft
2 m — 6 ft
— 5 ft
— 4 ft
1 m — 3 ft
— 2 ft
— 1 ft

'Handel'
~

This large-flowered climber, introduced in 1965, grows 3.6–4.5m (12–15ft) tall. The hot-pink-edged, cream-coloured, 9cm (3½in) flowers are double with a high-centred form. Mildly fragrant, this rose blooms in mid-season and is recurrent. The leaves are dark green with a copper cast, borne on thorny, vigorous canes. It is winter hardy, but somewhat prone to mildew.

'Jeanne Lajoie'
~

A climbing miniature introduced in 1975, this rose has small (2.5–4cm/1–1½in), double, light-pink flowers. The petals appear veined in a slightly paler pink. A good way to use miniature climbers is to lateral the canes along a fence, producing abundant blooms. Do not prune except to remove dead or unproductive wood.

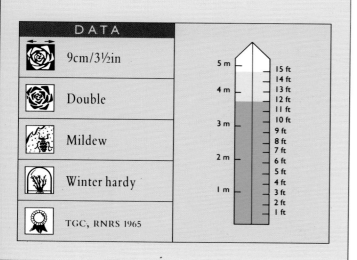

DATA

🌹	9cm/3½in
🌹	Double
🐛	Mildew
🌱	Winter hardy
🏵	TGC, RNRS 1965

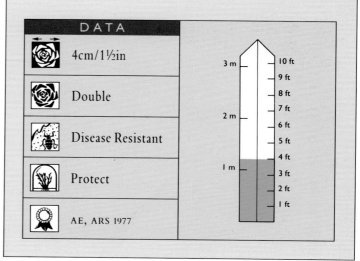

DATA

🌹	4cm/1½in
🌹	Double
🐛	Disease Resistant
🌱	Protect
🏵	AE, ARS 1977

'Margot Koster'

~

A climbing sport of the polyantha 'Margot Koster', introduced in 1935, this rose is often grafted as the top variety creating a large cascading tree. The 2.5–4cm (1–1½in) semi-double flowers are a coral to orange blended with pale yellow and white. Blooming mid to late-season, it is recurrent. The leaves are greyish-green. This rose is a vigorous plant, with canes reaching 3m (10ft) in length. It is disease resistant, but the climbing form needs some winter protection in colder areas.

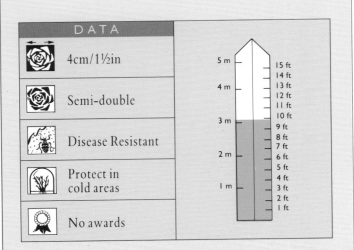

DATA	
4cm/1½in	5 m — 15 ft / 14 ft / 13 ft
Semi-double	4 m — 12 ft / 11 ft
Disease Resistant	3 m — 10 ft / 9 ft / 8 ft / 7 ft
Protect in cold areas	2 m — 6 ft / 5 ft / 4 ft / 1 m — 3 ft / 2 ft
No awards	1 ft

'Nymphenburg'

~

A pillar rose introduced in 1954, this is a vigorous shrub, growing up to 2.4m (8ft). The 10cm (4in), fragrant, semi-double, recurrent, salmon-pink flowers are slightly yellow at the base of the petals and are in clusters. An upright, well-branched shrub, it has medium-green large leaves and relatively smooth canes. It is disease resistant, but not consistently winter hardy.

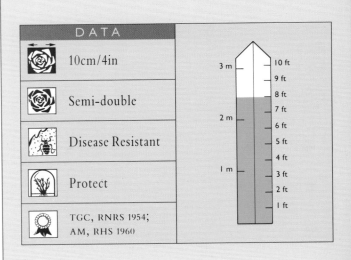

DATA	
10cm/4in	3 m — 10 ft / 9 ft / 8 ft
Semi-double	2 m — 7 ft / 6 ft / 5 ft
Disease Resistant	4 ft / 1 m — 3 ft
Protect	2 ft / 1 ft
TGC, RNRS 1954; AM, RHS 1960	

'Raymond Chenault'
~

A kordesii hybrid climber, this rose is quite vigorous, growing to 3m–3.6m (10–12ft). The large 10cm (4in) scarlet-red flowers are semi-double, growing in clusters. Fragrant and free-flowering, it blooms mid-season and is recurrent. The foliage is glossy, dark green. This rose is disease resistant and moderately winter hardy.

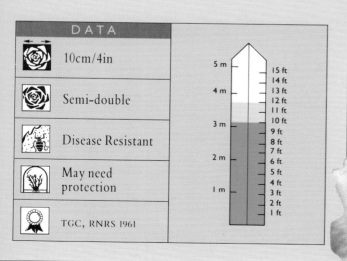

DATA	
10cm/4in	
Semi-double	
Disease Resistant	5 m — 15 ft / 14 ft
	4 m — 13 ft / 12 ft / 11 ft
	3 m — 10 ft / 9 ft
May need protection	2 m — 8 ft / 7 ft / 6 ft / 5 ft
	1 m — 4 ft / 3 ft / 2 ft / 1 ft
TGC, RNRS 1961	

HIGHLY RECOMMENDED CLIMBING AND RAMBLER ROSES

RED
'Altissimo'
'Chevy Chase'
'Don Juan'
'Dublin Bay'

BLEND
'America'
'First Prize'
'Handel'
'Over the Rainbow'
'Royal Sunset'

PINK
'Blossomtime'
'Cécile Brunner'
'Dainty Bess'
'Jeanne Lajoie'
'Rosarium Uetersen'

YELLOW
'Lawrence Johnston'

WHITE
'Sombreuil'

TOP TO BOTTOM 'Don Juan' and 'Jeanne Lajoie' are highly recommended climbing roses.
~

MINIATURE ROSES

Miniature roses are natural dwarf varieties, descended from an ancient Chinese dwarf rose. They were brought from China to Europe in the 1700s. They enjoyed a brief period of popularity in England and France in the early 1800s, where they were known as 'fairy' roses. Interest in miniatures soon declined and they were treated as horticultural curiosities for nearly a century. In 1918, the miniature *Rosa rouletii* was found in a Swiss village. It was soon crossed with hybrid and species roses and the world discovered the beauty of miniatures. There are now more than 400 varieties of miniature rose, with more being developed every year.

Miniatures have all the attributes of large roses in Lilliputian proportions. The flowers rarely exceed 4cm (1½in). The plants range from 7.5 to 45cm (3 to 18in), with an average height of 30cm (12in). They would certainly be dwarfed in the midst of a rose garden, but their diminutive forms are perfect for a low border, as bedding plants, in rock gardens, and in containers. They can successfully be grown year-round indoors as long as they receive plenty of sunlight. The flowers come in a wide range of colours. Their habit is generally bushy and spreading.

ABOVE The miniature rose 'Rise 'n' Shine' has been used here as an effective and attractive ground cover.
~

'Chipper'
~

Introduced in 1966, this variety has been consistently popular for 25 years. The 3cm (1¼in) salmon-pink flowers are double with a cupped form. This rose blooms mid-season with excellent repeat bloom. There is a very light fragrance. Growing 25–36cm (10–14in) tall, it is vigorous with an upright, well-branched habit. The foliage is dark green and glossy. It is a disease resistant and winter hardy rose.

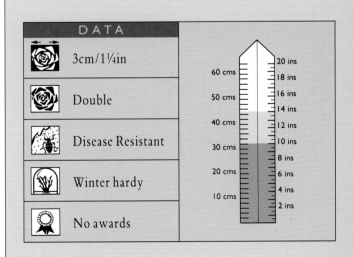

DATA	
🌹	3cm/1¼in
🌹	Double
	Disease Resistant
	Winter hardy
	No awards

60 cms	20 ins
	18 ins
50 cms	16 ins
40 cms	14 ins
	12 ins
30 cms	10 ins
	8 ins
20 cms	6 ins
	4 ins
10 cms	2 ins

'Cupcake'
~

Introduced in 1981, this rose was hybridized by an amateur. The very double, 4cm (1½in) flowers are medium pink and high-centred, with only a very faint fragrance. It blooms mid-season and is recurrent. A vigorous plant, it has a compact, bushy habit. The foliage is medium green and semi-glossy. This rose is disease resistant but needs some winter protection.

'Debut'
~

Introduced in 1989, this is a showy miniature. The 4cm (1½in) double flowers are crimson-red blended with creamy white at the base of the petals. As the flower opens, it becomes increasingly deeper in colour. It flowers mid-season and is everblooming. A vigorous plant growing to 38cm (15in), it has a bushy habit. It is disease resistant and winter hardy. It makes a splashy border or low hedge.

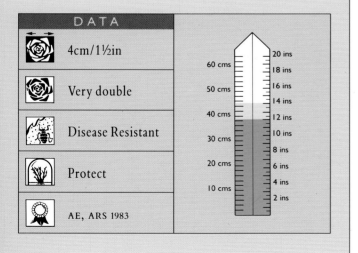

DATA	
4cm/1½in	
Very double	
Disease Resistant	
Protect	
AE, ARS 1983	

DATA	
4cm/1½in	
Double	
Disease Resistant	
Winter hardy	
AARS 1989	

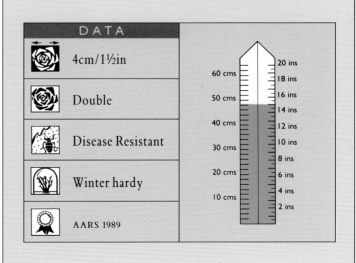

'Hotline'
~

Introduced in 1984, this miniature is a bit too vigorous for a container, but works well in a garden bed or border. The medium-red flowers are 4cm (1½in) wide and semi-double. This rose blooms mid-season and repeats well. The flower is high-centred, becoming cupped when open. A miniature moss rose, it has a pine fragrance. It is compact, reaching 38–45cm (15–18in), but strong growing and very vigorous. The medium-green foliage is semi-glossy. It is disease resistant and winter hardy.

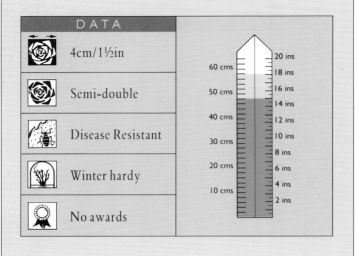

DATA	
🌹	4cm/1½in
🌹	Semi-double
🐞	Disease Resistant
🌱	Winter hardy
🏅	No awards

60 cms — 20 ins
— 18 ins
50 cms — 16 ins
— 14 ins
40 cms — 12 ins
30 cms — 10 ins
— 8 ins
20 cms — 6 ins
— 4 ins
10 cms — 2 ins

'Jean Kenneally'
~

This miniature, popular as an exhibition variety, was introduced in 1984. The 4cm (1½in) double flowers are an apricot blend. It has the classic hybrid tea-type form with a high-centred flower. It blooms mid-season and is an excellent repeat bloomer. An upright plant with a well-branched, bushy habit, it grows from 25 to 36cm (10 to 14in) tall. The medium-green leaves are semi-glossy. It is disease resistant and winter hardy.

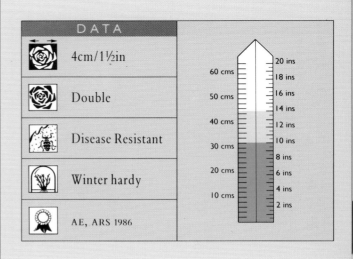

DATA	
🌹	4cm/1½in
🌹	Double
🐞	Disease Resistant
🌱	Winter hardy
🏅	AE, ARS 1986

60 cms — 20 ins
— 18 ins
50 cms — 16 ins
— 14 ins
40 cms — 12 ins
30 cms — 10 ins
— 8 ins
20 cms — 6 ins
— 4 ins
10 cms — 2 ins

'Magic Carrousel'
~

Introduced in 1972, this miniature is an attention-grabber. The large (for a miniature), 4.5–5cm (1¾–2in), semi-double flowers are white with rosy-red edges. The flowers are a cupped form, opening almost flat. It blooms mid-season and is recurrent. The light fragrance is reminiscent of violets. A very vigorous shrub, it grows 38–45cm (15–18in) tall, but has been known to grow as tall as 75cm (30in). The semi-glossy leaves are bronze-green. It is disease resistant and winter hardy.

DATA	
5cm/2in	
Semi-double	
Disease Resistant	
Winter hardy	
AE, ARS 1975	

'Over the Rainbow'
~

This bicolor miniature was introduced in 1972. The 3–4cm (1¼–1½in) double flowers are cerise-red blended with yellow. The upper sides of the pointed petals are yellow at the base, with red dominating; the reverse sides of the petals are dominant yellow blending into red. The lightly fragrant flowers are borne in clusters. This rose blooms continuously from mid-season. A vigorous plant with an upright, well-branched habit, it grows to 36cm (14in) tall. The dark-green leaves are semi-glossy. It is disease resistant and winter hardy.

DATA	
4cm/1½in	
Double	
Disease Resistant	
Winter hardy	
AE, ARS 1975	

'Rainbow's End'
~

Introduced in 1984, this miniature is versatile, growing well indoors or out. The 4cm (1½in) double flowers are a yellow blend. The very lightly scented flowers have a high-centred form. This rose blooms mid-season and repeats well. Growing 25–36cm (10–14in) tall, it has a bushy, well-branched, upright habit. The dark-green leaves are glossy. It is disease resistant and winter hardy.

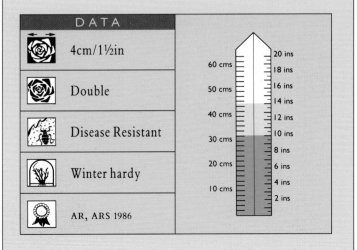

DATA	
4cm/1½in	
Double	
Disease Resistant	
Winter hardy	
AR, ARS 1986	

60 cms / 20 ins
50 cms / 18 ins
40 cms / 16 ins
30 cms / 14 ins
20 cms / 12 ins
10 cms / 10 ins / 8 ins / 6 ins / 4 ins / 2 ins

'Rise 'n' Shine'
~

Introduced in 1977, this is one of the best yellow miniatures. The 4cm (1½in) bright-yellow flowers are double with a high-centred form. It blooms mid-season and repeats well. The fragrance is light. It grows 25–36cm (10–14in) tall with a rounded, upright, bushy habit. The leaves are dark green.

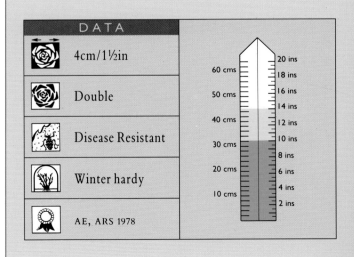

DATA	
4cm/1½in	
Double	
Disease Resistant	
Winter hardy	
AE, ARS 1978	

60 cms / 20 ins
50 cms / 18 ins
40 cms / 16 ins
30 cms / 14 ins
20 cms / 12 ins
10 cms / 10 ins / 8 ins / 6 ins / 4 ins / 2 ins

'Yellow Doll'
~

Introduced in 1962, this miniature is outstanding for its relatively large flowers. It is a small, compact, bushy rose, growing from 20–25cm (8–10in) tall. By contrast, the clear yellow flowers are 4cm (1½in) wide. The double flowers have a high-centred form, and are mildly fragrant. It blooms in mid-season and repeats well. A climbing form is also available, growing to 1.2m (4ft). The deep-green leaves appear leathery. It is disease resistant and winter hardy.

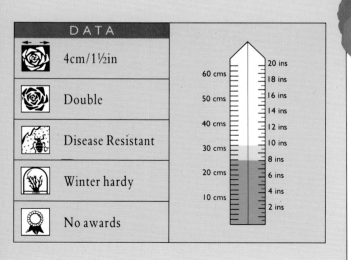

DATA	
4cm/1½in	
Double	
Disease Resistant	
Winter hardy	
No awards	

HIGHLY RECOMMENDED MINIATURES

RED
'Beauty Secret'
'Orange Sunblaze'
'Rose Hills Red'
'Starina'
'Top Secret'

YELLOW
'Rise 'n' Shine'
'Yellow Doll'

WHITE
'Little Eskimo'
'Simplex'
'Snow Bride'
'White Angel'

PINK
'Baby Betsy McCall'
'Cuddles'
'Cupcake'
'Judy Fischer'
'Swedish Doll'

MAUVE
'Lavender Jewel'

BLEND
'Dreamglo'
'Holy Toledo'
'Mary Marshall'
'Party Girl'
'Peaches 'n' Cream'

TOP TO BOTTOM 'Rise 'n' Shine', *'Yellow Doll' and 'Cupcake' are highly recommended miniature roses.*
~

GLOSSARY

ACID SOIL   Soil with a pH value of less than 7.0 (neutral).

ALKALINE SOIL   Soil with a pH value of more than 7.0 (neutral).

ANCHOR ROOT   A large root whose main purpose is to hold the plant in the ground.

ANTHER   The upper part of the stamen which holds the pollen sacs.

BALLING   A condition in which the outer petals cling together, preventing the rose from opening. It usually occurs during wet, cool weather.

BARE ROOT   A dormant plant without any soil around the roots.

BASAL CANE   A large cane on a rose bush that originates at the bud union.

BICOLOUR   A two-coloured rose, most commonly with one colour on the outside of the petal and another on the inside.

BLEND   Two or more colours that meld into one another on both sides of the petals.

BUD   (1) A partly opened flower. (2) A small swelling or projection on a plant that will develop into a flower, leaf or shoot. (3) *See* **bud eye.**

BUD EYE   A dormant bud found on the stem just above a leaf attachment (axil) or a leaf scar. Sometimes called a bud or eye.

BUD UNION   The swollen area of the stem where the rootstock and top variety were grafted. Found between 5cm (2in) above and below soil level, depending on the climate.

BUDDING   Propagation from a bud eye.

BUTTON CENTRE   In very double roses, a round centre formed by unopened petaloids.

CALYX   Collectively, the sepals of a flower.

CALYX TUBE   A tube formed by the base of the sepals and the receptacle.

CANE   One of the main stems of a rose bush, originating at the bud union.

CLONE   A plant that has been reproduced vegetatively from the parent plant and has the same genetic make-up and hence appearance.

CONFUSED CENTRE   The centre of a flower with petals in no pattern; a disorganized centre.

COROLLA   Collectively, the petals of a flower.

CORYMB   A flat-topped flower cluster with individual buds emerging at different points on the axis, it blooms from the edges towards the centre.

CROWN   The area of the bud union, near the soil level, where the top variety and rootstock are grafted.

CUPPED   A rose with the petals open so that the centre and stamens are visible.

CUTTING   A method of propagation whereby a portion of the plant, usually the stem, is induced to form roots and, therefore, a new plant.

DEAD-HEADING   Removal of spent flowers from a bush, encouraging formation of new flowers rather than seed formation.

DIEBACK   A stem or cane that has died from cold temperatures or a pruning wound.

DISBUD   To remove side (secondary) buds on a main flowering stem to produce a larger primary flower.

DORMANT   The state in which a plant is not actively growing, although it is still alive. Dormancy usually occurs in winter, as a way of surviving cold or drought.

DOUBLE   A flower with 24 to 50 petals.

EYE   *See* **bud eye.**

FEEDER ROOT   A small root that absorbs moisture and nutrients from the surrounding soil.

FILAMENT   The thread-like stalk of the stamen that bears the anther.

FOLIAR FEED   The application of a water soluble, non-burning fertilizer directly to the leaves of a plant.

GENUS   (plural genera) A collection of species that have certain characteristics in common.

HEEL IN   A temporary planting, covering the roots with moist soil until the plant can be properly planted.

HIGH-CENTRED   The classic form of a hybrid tea rose, with the central petals longest.

HIP   The fruit of a rose, usually brightly coloured, and formed from the ripened receptacle.

HYBRID   A plant that is the result of cross-pollination of two species or varieties, either in the wild or in cultivation.

LATERAL   A branch of a basal (main) cane; also called a lateral cane.

LAYERING   A method of propagation whereby a low growing stem is partially cut on the underside and pegged into the soil. The layer is separated from the parent plant once roots are established.

LEAF   In a rose, a compound leaf, composed of an odd number (usually three, five or seven) leaflets attached to the stem below an eye.

LEAF AXIL   The angle between the leaf stalk (petiole) and the stem.

LEAFLET   The leaf-like parts that make up a compound leaf. On roses, leaflets are arranged in opposite pairs with a single leaflet at the tip.

MAIN SHOOT   A basal cane or vigorous lateral cane.

MUDDLED CENTRE   The same as a confused centre, usually referring to old garden roses.

MULCH   A layer of organic, or inorganic, matter that is applied to the surface of the soil to suppress weeds, conserve moisture and protect from weather extremes.

OVARY   The swollen area at the base of the pistil where seeds develop.

PEG   A method for holding long canes to the ground, as for winter protection, by attaching the end of the cane to a peg in the soil.

PETAL   The parts of a flower that are within the sepals and surround the pistils and stamens. They are usually coloured, and as a unit are called the corolla.

PETALOID   Very short petals at the centre of a flower.

PETIOLE   The leaf stalk.

pH   A scale of hydrogen ion concentration from 1.0–14.0, indicating relative acid and alkaline values.

PHOTOSYNTHESIS   The process in plants whereby the green parts manufacture oxygen and carbohydrates in the presence of sunlight, from the water and carbon dioxide of the atmosphere.

PISTIL   The female reproductive organ of a flower, composed of the ovary, style (stalk) and stigma.

PRICKLE   A thorn; usually a small thorn.

QUARTERED   The petals of a flower arranged in three, four or five segments.

RECEPTACLE   The enlarged upper end of the flower stalk on which the flower forms and grows.

RECURRENT   Continuous bloom. Also referred to as remontant.

REFLEXED   A backward-bending petal.

REMONTANT   *See* **recurrent.**

REVERSE   The back side of a petal.

RHACHIS   The stem-like portion of a compound leaf to which the leaflets are attached.

ROOTSTOCK   The rose that is used as the root system in a grafted rose.

SCION   A shoot or bud, usually removed for the purpose of planting, budding or grafting.

SELF-CLEANING   A flower that breaks up naturally and falls to the ground.

SELF-POLLINATION   The transfer of pollen from the anthers to the stigmas of the same flower, or to the stigmas or another flower on the same plant.

SEMI-DOUBLE   A flower with 12 to 23 petals.

SEPAL   The individual leaf-like parts of the calyx, usually green in colour.

SINGLE   (1) A flower with five to 11 petals. (2) A variety having only one bloom per stem.

SPORT   A naturally occurring mutation of a plant.

STAMEN   The male reproductive part of a flower, composed of the filament with the anther at the tip.

STEM   The branch of a cane which develops from a bud eye, that has leaves and at least one flower.

STIGMA   The tip of the style of a flower, which becomes sticky and receives pollen.

STIPULE   The leaf-like parts at the base of the petiole.

STYLE   The slender, stalk-like part between the stigma and ovary.

SUCKER   A shoot that originates from the rootstock, which is noticeably different from the shots of the top variety.

TOP VARIETY   The rose that is used for its canes, stems and flowers in a grafted rose.

UNDERSTOCK   *See* **rootstock.**

VARIETIES   A unit below either that of a species or subspecies that shows minor differences from either of these. Varieties are often of greater horticultural significance than of botanical importance.

VERY DOUBLE   A flower with more than 50 petals.

INDEX

Numbers in *italic* refer to illustration captions

Numbers in **bold** refer to rose entries in the A–Z section.

CREDITS

*All photography by the author, Cathy Wilkinson Barash, with the
exception of the following: British Library, page 6; Scala, Florence,
page 7; Osterreichische Nationalbibliothek, Vienna, page 8; Harris
Museum, Preston, page 9; Quarto Publishing, pages 10, 11, 44 r
(photo. Ian Howes), 48/49 (photo. Paul Forrester); Harry Smith
Horticultural Collection, jacket. Illustrations on pages 13, 27 and 40
by Bill Barash; all other illustrations by Danny McBride.*